City Breaks
in
Rome
– a new look

REG BUTLER

In Association with

THOMSON HOLIDAYS

SETTLE PRESS

Text © 1994 Reg Butler
Second Edition 1997

First published by Settle Press
10 Boyne Terrace Mews
London W11 3LR

ISBN (Paperback) 1 872876 53 6

Printed by Villiers Publications
19 Sylvan Avenue
London N3 2LE

Foreword

As Britain's leading short breaks specialist, we recognise the need for detailed information and guidance for City Break travellers. But much more is required than just a listing of museums and their opening times. For a few days, the City Break visitor wants to experience the local continental lifestyle.

Reg Butler has had considerable experience of the great Italian cities. As a young courier, he conducted ten full seasons of grand European tours, with regular visits to Venice, Florence and Rome. Since then he has returned many times to Italy, writing travel articles for British and American newspapers and magazines.

For this book, Reg Butler collaborated closely with our resident Thomson staff, who have year-round experience of helping visitors enjoy these cities. We're sure you'll find this book invaluable in planning how to make best personal use of your time.

In this revised edition, all opening hours, prices, phone numbers and restaurant recommendations have been checked by Thomson's resident office staff and reps in Rome. They have the huge advantage of being able to monitor changes as they happen. But, inevitably, more changes will occur between the date of printing and when the reader travels.

As well as City Breaks in Italy, other books in the series cover Paris, Amsterdam, Central Europe, Spain, New York, Dublin, Bruges and Brussels. Thomson also operate to many other world cities from departure points across the UK.

THOMSON CITYBREAKS

Contents

Chapter One

The magic of Rome

Rome has enough sightseeing to keep you busy for weeks: ancient ruins, miles of colossal city walls, catacombs and churches, monuments and fountains around every corner. Yet, amid this setting of dramatic remains from the past, the modern Roman exults in the 20th century.

There is no looking backwards, for instance, in the postwar architecture of Rome. As you travel into town from the airport, your first view of Rome is ultra-modern: pastel-coloured apartments on the city outskirts.

Likewise in central Rome, look at the ultra-modern Termini Railway Station, with its dramatically cantilevered roof that makes one gasp with its daring and imagination.

Yet away to one side, left untouched as an integral part of the architect's plan, is a large section of original Roman wall, built 2000 years ago. That sight is symbolic. It reminds us that the Rome of today mixes quite well with the Rome of ancient history.

Going round central Rome is like travelling on a Time Machine. There are columns which stood there when Julius Caesar was just back from conquering Britain; the jail where St Peter was locked up; the tower of a medieval palace, a facade by Michelangelo, or a church by Bernini; the balcony from which Mussolini declared war on Britain.

As the capital of the Catholic world, Vatican City is a place of pilgrimage to millions every year. Even to non-Catholics, there is great sense of awe on those occasions when the Pope emerges at noon onto his balcony, and blesses all the thousands

7

INTRODUCTION

gathered below in St Peter's Square. And you think of all the pilgrim millions who have likewise been blessed over the centuries...

A visit to Rome is a journey into the past, greatly enlivened by the present.

"When in Rome, do as the Romans do."

Such as? Well, just like anywhere else, the local inhabitants eat, drink, chase girls and enjoy themselves. Doing all that in Roman style is good enough formula for a holiday to remember.

But, first, what about the monuments?

Of course, for a 20th-century Roman, all the guide-book sights are just part of the normal background scenery, scattered throughout the city.

Zipping through the Borghese Gardens, a Fiat-driver takes the fast route that runs beside the towering walls of ancient Rome – as well-preserved and impressive as 2,000 years ago.

He whirls though the Pincio Gate with all the courage and driving skill of a Roman charioteer, and thence down Via Veneto to Piazza Barberini, and so across central Rome. En route, there are ancient Roman columns and ruined temples – 17th-century fountains and Renaissance churches – palaces, museums and art galleries. It's an incredibly rich cultural diet which a modern Roman absorbs over a lifetime.

The footsore tourist, struggling to 'do' Rome in three days, often ends with mental indigestion. The best policy for first-time visitors is to take the standard city sightseeing by coach. After morning and afternoon sessions – several hours with a knowledgeable guide pouring forth history, facts, dates, anecdotes – most tourists then feel limp.

But at least the cream has been skimmed: Colosseum, Forum, Vatican City, Pantheon and a few churches. You can then return at leisure to whatever interests you most. But you cannot possibly see everything in detail!

Typical is the guided sightseeing through the Vatican Museums – certainly the world's richest.

Some of the guides for one-day Rome marshall their flocks outside the entrance just before opening time. Then, to keep ahead, they march briskly through several hundrd yards of halls and galleries lined with masterpieces of art and sculpture, collected by the Popes over long centuries.

Anyone who pauses a moment must break into a trot to catch up. The aim is to reach the Sistine Chapel before all the other tour groups make movement difficult. Obviously the daily Sistine Chapel stampede is ludicrous. But if you want to linger among the fabulous treasures of the Vatican Museum, it's quite simple to return at your own pace; or to take a guided tour which just concentrates on that Museum alone.

Once you have the overall view, just relax and enjoy your own discoveries. Routes across central Rome to the principal monuments are signposted for walkers. Regrettably, every Roman car-owner prefers to drive, leading to massive traffic jams and long-term problems of exhaust pollution.

Many of the famous monuments and buildings are currently being cleaned and restored. It's an endless task, slowed by lack of funds. Many tourist sights have been draped in scaffolding for several years. But fortunately Rome still has plenty left.

One of the great pleasure spots of Rome is the entire area around the Spanish Steps – a sociable gathering point for tourists and Romans alike.

If you're in Rome during the Spring Festival in April, spend an hour at the Spanish Steps, specially decorated top to bottom with massed flowers. That's when Romans outnumber tourists around Spanish Square. All the weekend brides go there for group photographs – entire wedding parties, one after another, to pose against a gorgeous background of azaleas. Pack plenty of colour film!

Finally, it's a complete evening entertainment to go down to the Trevi Fountain to look at all the visitors, busy throwing coins into the water to ensure a return trip to Rome.

That's where the young men of Rome go girl-hunting among the ever-changing supply of talent. With traffic jammed by horse-carriages, the Trevi Fountain becomes starting-point for international flirtations. It's all part of the magic of Rome!

Chapter Two
The road to Rome

2.1 When to go

Part of the Rome is a city for all seasons. Spring-time, especially at Easter, the big rush starts. In the hotter summer months, when midday temperatures can reach 90° F, many sightseers adopt the good Italian tradition of an afternoon siesta. It's not a "waste" of time. You are then refreshed for a cooler return to the sightseeing circuits, followed by the tranquil pleasures of open-air dining, watching the world go by from pavement cafés or attending open-air opera.

Autumn is well worth considering, for easier progress around the sites. Finally, let's remember that, during the days of the Grand Tour, the illustrious travellers of the 18th and 19th centuries regularly wintered in Rome. December onwards, the musical and social scene is in full swing, offering a different picture from the Rome of high summer.

Average temperatures go from 45°F in January, to 57°F in April, 77°F in July, or 62°F in October.

In fact, any long weekend can be a good time to visit the Italian capital. Out-of-pocket expenses are quite reasonable. At least a hundred valid reasons exist for a civilised human being to sample the cultural and scenic riches that Italy can offer. Quite apart from the cultural scene, Rome is a place to enjoy yourself and have fun.

Of course, in a brief visit, it's impossible to absorb more than a tiny fraction of Rome's potential in a single trip. The only solution is to limit yourself to a selection of the highlights, and leave the rest till "next time".

2.2 Airports

Let's clarify first that Rome has two international airports. Most visitors on charter flights into Ciampino Airport from Gatwick or Manchester usually have a transfer included to their chosen hotel.

Otherwise, go-it-alone travellers on British Airways or Alitalia scheduled services will arrive at Fiumicino airport, also known as Leonardo da Vinci, 23 miles from the city centre.

If you are fending for yourself, you'll find that taxis into town are expensive, at around £34. There is a taxi information office at the airport, where you can enquire about ordering a taxi, and the approximate fare.

Instead, the best policy is to use the train services which operate into central Rome. About once an hour there's a direct service to and from Termini Station, costing 13,000 lire for the 30-minute journey.

A local train, stopping at many stations en route, arrives at Tiburtina (on the B Line Metro) in 40 minutes, and costing 7,000 lire. Either way is faster than the road journey which can take an hour, depending on traffic jams.

From the arrival station, treat yourself to a taxi. Avoid using taxi drivers who approach you – they are usually unofficial and unreliable. 'Official' taxis are always yellow or white, and have a meter.

Alternatively, if you have pinpointed that your hotel is located near a Metro station, venture on the subway system (details see below).

2.3 Your hotel

Check-in: Normal check-in and check-out time is midday, but confirm with reception. If you arrive before noon, you may check in and leave luggage with reception until your room is free. If your final departure is after midday, pack your cases before going out for the morning and leave them in the left-luggage room.

ARRIVAL IN ROME

Electricity: Italian electricity is 220 volts. Plugs are generally Continental-style two-pin. Pack a plug adaptor if you expect to use your own electric gadgets.

Lighting: Hotel corridors sometimes have a time switch for the lights, long enough to unlock your door. Look for a small orange light and press the button.

Water taps: 'C' stands for *caldo*, meaning hot; 'F' is *freddo*, meaning cold.

Breakfast: Italian breakfasts are modest Continental – bread or rolls, jam or marmalade, a scraping of butter, and tea or coffee. Normally it's served early, available between 7.30 and 9.30.

Tipping: Around 1,000 lire per case is usual for porters. Chambermaids will appreciate the lire you leave for them in the bedroom at the end of your stay.

2.4 Getting around in Rome

Rome on foot

Central Rome still keeps a human dimension to its buildings. The little squares and piazzas ring to the sound of children, while hundreds of tourists during the season find that exploring Rome on foot is the easiest way to get around.

With pedestrians in mind, many street corners have signs pointing the way for walkers to reach the principal sites and locations. Because of the one-way traffic system and the huge traffic jams, walking is often much faster than going by car.

Driving in Rome is an adventure in itself. As the traffic lights get near to turning green, the Fiat legions charge as though in hot pursuit of barbarians. They drive like kamikaze fighter pilots in a dog-fight – wing to wing, swerving and lane-changing, accelerating fast and then jamming on the brakes with another quick swerve to avoid crossfire from side turnings.

Traffic lights are a laugh. Red means go if you think you can make it. If you're thinking of sightseeing around Rome in a self-drive car – forget it!

Most visitors are pleasantly surprised at how easily Rome can be explored on foot. Cover Rome sector by sector, exploring the most famous sites and monuments that are conveniently close together. But carry a small supply of bus or Metro tickets, to avoid having to walk home.

Metro

This is the fastest way of getting across Rome, unhindered by surface traffic. It's worth taking a few minutes to learn the system. However, there are only two lines. Check whether your hotel is reasonably close.

Line A – see below – can be especially useful in linking up several major tourist locations. Hours of operation are 06.30 to midnight.

Tickets – equally valid for buses and trams – costing 1500 lire can be bought from:
• Newsagents/Tabacchi with signs saying 'ATAC abbonamento bus metro'.
• Automatic vending machines in Metro or bus stations. Make sure you have plenty of coins.
• Counters in Termini, Lepanto and Ottaviano stations.

Combined day tickets called "Big" for Metro and buses can be purchased from ATAC kiosks situated at bus terminals, or from ticket counters in the above mentioned Metro stations. Price 6000 lire. A weekly pass is also available.

Using the system

There are two lines, which cross handily at Termini Station:

Line A – from Via Ottaviano (near Vatican City), Flaminio (Piazza del Popolo), Piazza di Spagna and Piazza Barberini to Termini Station and thence to Cinecittà and Anagnina.

Line B – from Termini Station via Colosseum, Massimo (for Circus Maximus and Caracalla Baths), Piramide, to San Paolo fuori le Mura and thence to EUR. Going north-east from Termini Station, Line B serves Castro Pretorio and Tiburtina (for a train to Fiumicino airport).

ARRIVAL IN ROME

Metro entrances are marked with a red M. One ticket takes you anywhere on Line A or B. Entry to platforms is via automatic barriers. Work out which way to go (only a choice of two!) by reading the direction lists on the platform, showing the subsequent stops.

Doors open automatically. If the Metro is crowded, stay close to the doors. To wriggle your way out, say "Permesso".

Most important: BEWARE OF PICKPOCKETS.

Buses

Hours of operation: 5 a.m. until midnight, but some buses run only between 9 and 21 hrs. There are also very limited night services – 'servizio notturna' – but they do generally run as advertised.

Tickets cost 1,500 lire for 75 minutes, using the same tickets as the Metro. These are bought in advance from newspaper stands or tobacconists that display a white sign saying ATAC, with the picture of a bus; or from Vendita Biglietti kiosks at bus terminals.

Best buy is the one-day 'Big' ticket – details in Metro section above. For longer-stay visitors, consider the weekly pass – available only from the ATAC sales kiosk in front of Termini Station.

Using the system

Bus stops are yellow and called FERMATA. If the word RICHIESTA appears on the bus-stop sign, this means 'request' and you must raise your arm to halt the bus. If in doubt, put your arm out anyway.

There's a list of stops under each bus number. While waiting, always check to see whether it says FERIALE as this means the bus runs only on work days. So, if it's Sunday, you'll have to wait until Monday to catch it.

Board at the back of the bus, and punch your ticket in the time-dating machine. You can change onto a connecting bus, using the same ticket within the valid period of 75 minutes. But you cannot switch between bus and Metro on the same ticket.

If the bus is crowded, then start moving towards the middle door a couple of stops before you need to alight, saying 'Permesso' as you edge through. Ring bell to stop the bus.

Sorry to repeat ourselves, but **don't give pickpockets a chance.**

Taxis

Official taxis are yellow or white and should always have a working meter. If not, get out! The driver may then find that the meter is properly working, after all. There are many stands throughout the city. Here's where to find some of them:

- Top of Via Veneto
- In front of Termini Station
- In front of St Peter's Square
- Bottom of Spanish Steps
- Generally in main piazzas and tourist sites.

There are usually supplements payable on all taxi rides at night and at weekends, and for suitcases.

If a taxi is called for you from the hotel or a restaurant, the meter starts working from when the driver is called. It is quite difficult to get a taxi by hailing in the street, as empty cabs are often on a call.

N.B. If you have any doubts about your taxi, note down the licence number. Avoid using drivers who approach you, as they are usually unofficial, with no meters, and can scalp you on fares.

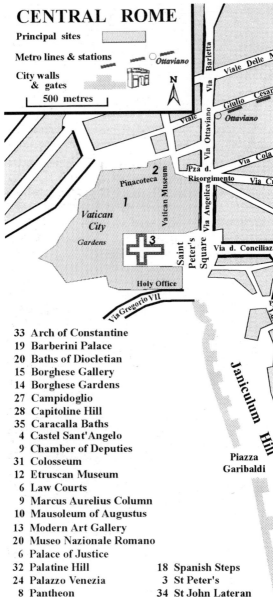

CENTRAL ROME

Principal sites

Metro lines & stations   Ottaviano

City walls & gates

500 metres

N

Barletta

Via

Viale Delle M

Giulio Cesare

Ottaviano

Via Ottaviano

Via Cola

Pza d. Risorgimento

Via Cr

Via Angelica

2 Vatican Museum

Pinacoteca

1

Vatican City

Gardens

3

Saint Peter's Square

Via d. Conciliazi

Holy Office

Via Gregorio VII

Janiculum Hill

Piazza Garibaldi

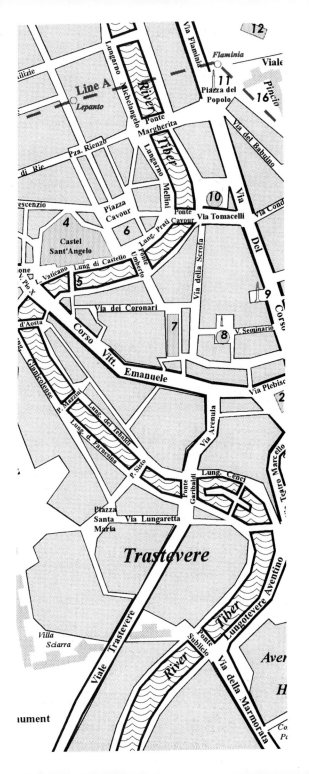

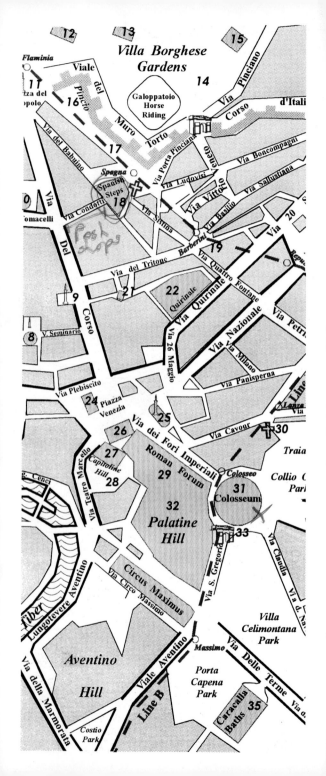

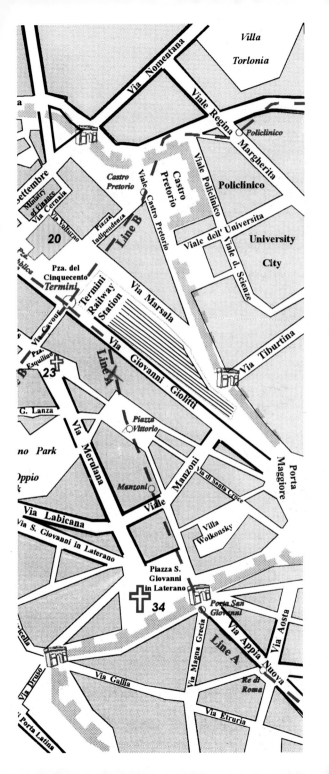

Chapter Three
Basic Rome

3.1 Planning your sightseeing

The amount of Roman sightseeing and historic interest is quite fantastic: ancient columns and ruined temples – 17th-century fountains and Renaissance churches – great palaces, museums and art galleries.

Outside the immense city walls are the ruined aqueducts, with their piers striding across the open countryside towards Rome, whence they brought all the water supplies for the ancient Imperial capital.

There is delight in following through the march of the centuries: noting the great pagan temples of the Roman Forum; conjuring up the wild and brutal Roman holidays in the Colosseum; plodding around the Caracalla Baths – one of the most grandiose buildings of 3rd-century Rome; exploring Catacombs that played such a big part in early Christian history; noting the blank spots – the Dark Ages when the barbarians took over.

All that is followed by seeing the great triumph of the Renaissance, when men created new expressions of faith and worship. For the art lover, the Vatican museums themselves are enough reason for visiting Rome.

Amid this embarrassment of sightseeing riches, don't panic that you're going to miss something. Just pick out the highlights which could interest you most, and leave the rest till your next visit.

Attune yourself to the Roman pattern of a latish lunch and a lengthy siesta. It's not a 'waste' of time. You awake refreshed for another bout of sightseeing and then the magic of Rome by night.

3.2 Essential Rome

Give yourself a year, and you can see everything in Rome. Otherwise, on an all-too-brief city break, at least try to cover the essentials:

• A morning at Vatican City and ending (if it's Sunday and the Pope's in town) with a Papal blessing at noon.

• Relax and enjoy the sight of other tourists at the Spanish Steps.

• From the Spanish Steps, explore Via Condotti and the surrounding luxury-shopping area, to gasp at the prices.

• Pay homage to Ancient Rome: Capitoline Hill, Roman and Imperial Forums and Colosseum.

• Stroll from the Pantheon to take-it-easy Piazza Navona, absorbing the atmosphere.

• Dine at a street restaurant in the Trastevere district.

• Tour the illuminations, by horse-carriage or motor coach.

• Cool off at the fountains of Villa d'Este, at Tivoli, 20 miles east of Rome.

• Enjoy a night at the opera: Teatro dell'Opera from December to June; Caracalla Baths July to mid-August.

• With another day to spare, dash off on the long but rewarding excursion to Naples, Pompeii and perhaps Sorrento.

Much of Basic Rome is covered by the City Tours offered by local travel agencies. The normal pattern is to divide the sightseeing into separate half-day Classical Rome and Vatican City tours.

Taking those orientation tours will give you the overall picture, rather than fumbling around on your own and possibly missing some of the great highlights. En route, the coach itineraries give an overview of the famous fountains, square and public monuments of the Historic Centre.

On the evening of arrival, seriously consider taking an Illuminations Tour, which gives a superb introduction to the magic of floodlit Rome. It makes a delightful appetizer for next day's sightseeing.

3.3 Sunday in Rome

There's plenty doing in Rome on a Sunday, except for dedicated shoppers. It can be idyllic for sight-seeing, with central Rome relatively clear of traffic. Pedestrians can walk around without being fumigated. Photo enthusiasts can step into the road for that better-composed picture, without being mown down by a passing Fiat.

Excursions

Why not sit back, and take a trip? Excursions available on a Sunday include the standard City Tours, half-day to Tivoli, or a very full day to Naples, Pompeii and Sorrento.

Shops & Markets

Regular shops are closed, but the Flea Market at Porta Portese in the Trastevere district is in full swing from 7.00-13.00 hrs.

Museums & Galleries

Most are open on Sundays – at least until lunchtime. Some national museums and galleries offer free entrance on one or two Sundays each month. Remember that many are closed on Mondays.

Church Services
St Peter's, Vatican City

High Altar at 09.00, 10.30, 12.15, 16.00 and 17.30 hrs.
San Guiseppe Altar at 11.00 and 13.00 hrs.
Capella del Sacramento at 11.30 hrs.
Altar Vespers at 17.00 hrs.

When the Pope is in residence, the Sunday Papal blessing is at 12.00 hrs at St Peter's, or at Castel Gandolfo outside Rome in peak summer months.

St Paul's Within the Walls

Via Nazionale   Anglican Mass 8.30 and 10.30 hrs.

Your representative can give details of other services in English.

Chapter Four

Ancient Rome

4.1 A glance at history

Thousands of learned volumes have been written on the history of Rome. Let's start with a 5-minute summary.

The area of present-day Rome was first settled around 1,000 BC. The advantages: here the Tiber could be forded, while the adjacent hills were free of malaria.

The opening chapters of Roman history are coloured by legend and folklore. The twin brothers, Romulus and Remus, are named as the mythological founders of Rome. When born, they were cast adrift on the Tiber, but were rescued by a friendly she-wolf who suckled them. There, at the foot of the Palatine Hill, the brothers were found and brought up by the shepherd Faustulus and his wife. Later, on 21st April 753 BC, the twins used a sacred plough to mark out the boundary of a new city. Each brother wanted to be ruler, with the city named after himself. Romulus murdered his brother, and reigned as king of Roma until 716 BC, when he disappeared in a clap of thunder.

As the lowest crossing point on the River Tiber – which was first bridged in the 7th century BC – Rome controlled the key trade routes between Etruria and Campania. Originally based on the Palatine Hill, the city expanded with fortifications across the neighbouring six hills – Capitoline, Viminal, Esquiline, Caelian, Aventine and Quirinal.

Two tribes – Latins and Sabines – came together in the city, and Rome soon outpaced other Latin cities in wealth. In late 7th century, the powerful

ANCIENT ROME

Etruscans to the northwest placed Etruscan kings on the Roman throne. During their reign, the swampy site of the Forum was drained, sewers were laid, a citadel and a temple were built on Capitoline Hill, defensive city walls were constructed and the Circus Maximus was laid out for horse racing.

Scandal erupted in 509 BC, when the Etruscan king's son raped Lucretia, a virtuous Roman lady. The indignant Romans overturned the Etruscan dynasty and proclaimed a Republic.

Innumerable wars were fought during the Republican period, with the Romans gradually expanding the territories they controlled throughout Italy, despite a setback in 390 BC when Rome was sacked by the Gauls. By diplomacy and military occupation, Roman power also spread beyond Italy.

Roman success in foreign wars brought riches to the capital, with the added bonus of cheap food – grain, wine and olive oil – from colonial territories. Thousands of slaves were imported to work the large landed estates.

The struggle for power in the 1st century BC – well dramatized by Shakespeare – finally led to the fall of the Republic in 31 BC, with Octavian taking the helm as Emperor in 23 BC, assuming the name of Caesar Augustus. He undertook a major rebuilding programme, became a great patron of the arts, and established the basis of Pax Romana – 200 years of peace and prosperity, when Rome had no rivals. The Empire was unified by the system of Roman roads, with good communications through a well-organised postal system.

Some Emperors were good, others very bad. But in general the city of Rome became steadily more magnificent, with marble monuments and buildings to glorify the name of each ruler. Large numbers of idlers and unemployed were kept out of mischief with bread and circuses. The splendour of Rome reached its peak in 2nd century AD.

Then came gradual decline, with the outposts of the Empire overrun by barbarians to the north, and Persians to the east. The 3rd century was a time of crisis with high taxation, inflation and a collapse in army discipline.

Turmoil and division

During the 50-year period from 235 to 284 AD, Rome had over two dozen emperors, of whom all bar one died violently.

History took a new turn under Constantine the Great, who ruled from 306 to 337 AD. He moved the capital of the Roman Empire to Byzantium, which he renamed Constantinople.

In 395 the Empire was permanently split between the Latin or Western Empire and the Byzantine or Eastern Empire. The latter survived until 1453, when Constantinople was finally overrun by the Turks and renamed Istanbul.

Meanwhile Rome was sacked by the Visigoths in the year 410 and the Vandals in 455, with an earthquake in between. These events marked the end of ancient Rome, with the city in ruins and deserted.

4.2 Remains of ancient Rome

The Capitol

To explore the main centre on your own, start from the Piazza Venezia, go right of the Victor Emmanuel Monument (the white wedding-cake which most Romans regard as an eyesore), and climb the broad flight of steps up to the Piazza del Campidoglio.

Although Capitoline Hill was the smallest of Rome's seven hills, it was the most important. On the southern peak of the hill stood the magnificent Temple of Jupiter, of which the remains can be seen in the Palazzo dei Conservatori.

Here were staged many of the big events of Roman history. When victorious generals returned from combat, they came in state procession to thank the gods. Here Brutus spoke, after the death of Julius Caesar.

On the northern summit was the Temple of Juno Moneta, close to the Roman mint, and now occupied by the church of Santa Maria d'Aracoeli.

The Piazza was remodelled by Michelangelo in 1536, with a superb 2nd-century equestrian statue of Marcus Aurelius on a central plinth. Modern pollution was destroying the bronze monument, until its removal in 1980 for renovation and rehousing in the adjacent Capitoline Museums.

Stop to visit the Museums if you want to see a great collection of Greek and Roman sculptures (see Chap 7). Otherwise, continue to the splendid viewpoint over ancient Rome, behind the Senator's Palace. The Palazzo dates in its present style from 1805, and houses Rome's town hall. This building – the medieval Senate House – saw the declaration of the Italian Republic in 1946, and signing of the European Community's Treaty of Rome in 1957.

Roman Forum

From the Capitol viewpoint, you have the best possible overall view of the original Forum. Below are the three Corinthian columns of the Temple of Vespasian, the Arch of Septimus Severus, and the remaining granite columns of the Temple of Saturn which dated from 497 BC and was used as the State Treasury like Fort Knox.

All the glory of the ancient Roman Forum – the scene of so many triumphant parades during the great days of the Empire – almost entirely disappeared during the Middle Ages. Columns and marble were carted off by medieval building contractors, rubble piled up, the drainage system collapsed, and the grass-covered site became the Cattle Field. Apart from spasmodic excavations, mainly in the hope of finding art treasures, the Forum was not explored again until the 19th century.

Take the flight of steps down (left of the Palazzo Senatorio) to reach the Via dei Fori Imperiali at the northwest corner of the Forum.

From there is choice of several routings. You could work northwards to peek over the railings around Caesar's Forum and then continue across the broad Via Dei Fori Imperiali to inspect Trajan's Forum, which includes Trajan's Column and the Market. Alternatively you could enter the Roman Forum itself, moving towards the Palatine Hill. Open 9 till sunset; Sun 9-13 hrs; Entrance 12,000 lire (free with UK passports for under-18s and over-60s). There's a convenient exit from the Palatine Hill, to reach the Colosseum.

Fori Imperiali, Street of the Imperial Forums

Rome outgrew the main Forum, so additions were made just north of the Foro Romano, along the line of Mussolini's Imperial Forums Way which leads from Piazza Venezia direct to the Colosseum. These extensions gave successive Emperors a status-symbol chance to vie with their predecessors, by trying to build an even more imposing addition. Judge for yourself. In date order, the contestants are:

Caesar's Forum (46 BC)

Here you can see the remains of a temple of Venus, intended to remind Romans that Julius Caesar claimed descent from the goddess. He used the premises to house his art collection. Close by is the site of the Mamertine Prison at the foot of the Capitoline Hill, where tradition says that St Peter was jailed. The prison is now a chapel called San Pietro in Carcere (St Peter in Prison), giving access to the gloomy dungeons where enemies of Rome were incarcerated. Christian martyrs are listed at the entrance.

Forum of Augustus (42 BC)

Built to commemorate Augustus's victory in 42 BC at Philippi, where he avenged the death of Julius Caesar (his adopted father) by the slaying of Cassius and Brutus. Still standing are three columns of the Temple of Mars Ultor – Mars the Avenger. The Forum included a statue of Augustus, seven times life-size, but only the footprints remain.

Nerva's Forum

All that remains are two Corinthian columns and the base of the Temple of Minerva.

Trajan's Forum (113 AD)

Posterity has given top rating to Trajan's Forum, especially remarkable for Trajan's Column which celebrated his victory over the Dacians (inhabitants of modern-day Romania).

A spiral frieze with over 100 scenes and 2500 figures winds its way up the 125-ft column. It forms a complete record of the campaign, depicting uniforms, weapons, siege operations and military techniques in faithful detail.

It's like a Bayeux Tapestry in marble, unrolling the story in sequence from bottom to top, originally in full colour that has long since faded. Aloft, a bronze statue of Trajan was exchanged in 1587 for the present statue of St Peter.

The site also has the remains of the 6-storey shopping centre, selling fruit and flowers on the ground floor; oil and wine on the 2nd; pepper and spices on 3rd and 4th. Social services were located on the 5th floor, with fish tanks fed by fresh- and salt-water aqueducts at roof level. Open: 9-19 hrs, Tue-Sat; Sun 9-13 hrs. Entrance: 3,750 lire.

Whichever routing you choose, you can end up at the Colosseum, which also has a convenient Metro station called Colosseo. Depending on your transport arrangements, the circuit can easily be followed in reverse.

Colosseum (80 AD)
One of Rome's most impressive buildings, inaugurated by Emperor Titus. Over 50,000 spectators seated in three tiers were able to watch gladiator fights, mock sea battles and the baiting and killing of wild beasts.

The upper tiers have been well restored, and there is plenty to see. Even the animal pens still exist, under the main floor. Most impressive are the enormous corridors through which thousands of spectators poured out after the show, emptying the Colosseum in ten minutes.
Open: 09.00 hrs to sunset. Wed & Hols, 9-13 hrs. Free entry, but 8,000 lire to visit the upper levels.

Arch of Constantine (315 AD)
Facing the Colosseum: the last great monument of ancient Rome was this triumphal Arch, built to mark a victory by Emperor Constantine over the rival Emperor Maxentius. Much of the decoration came from other monuments. Around the renovated Arch, archaeological digging is now under way.

Circo Massimo (Circus Maximus)

On the other side of the Palatine Hill, the Great Circus was built about 2nd century BC – former scene of chariot races. In its heyday, the Circus could hold 300,000 spectators. Successive emperors lavished funds on improvements and extensions. In the middle you can still see where the number of laps were recorded by the moving of 7 large wooden eggs on the central Spina, or dividing barrier. The circus fell into disuse after Rome fell.

Open daily. No entrance fee. Metro: Massimo.

Caracalla Baths (212 AD)

Located a ten-minute walk from the Circus Maximus, the enormous Caracalla Baths played a great part in the social life of Rome until the aqueducts were cut by Ostrogoth invaders in 546. Halls and galleries were of marble, and were decorated with marble and bronze sculptures, frescoes and mosaics. The well-stocked libraries carried all the best literature of Rome and Greece. The main swimming pool – the Tepidarium – could service 2,000 bathers at a time. The entire complex covers 27 acres, and the ruins continue to play a useful role as the backdrop to summer seasons of opera.

Open: 9 hrs till sunset except Mon and Holidays 9-13 hrs. Entrance 8,000 lire.

The Pantheon (80 AD)

A 'must' to visit, on Piazza della Rotonda. The Pantheon was reconstructed by Hadrian in 125 AD and converted into a church in the 7th century by Pope Boniface 1V. Raphael was buried here, and two Italian kings.

You enter through the original Roman bronze doors, but other bronze decorations were plundered. Within, the fantastic dome is still precisely as designed in Hadrian's time, with sunshine (or rain) pouring through a central opening called an oculus. Elements of the design have inspired innumerable architects over the centuries.

It's very pleasant to study the architecture from one of the Piazza bars facing the entrance.

Open: 9-17.30 hrs; Sun 9-13 hrs. No entrance fee.

ANCIENT ROME

Castel Sant'Angelo (135 AD)

On the Vatican side of the Tiber, facing Sant' Angelo Bridge, is the commanding presence of the Papal fortress which was originally intended as Hadrian's mausoleum. The bridge itself was also designed by Hadrian.

In 271 AD the mausoleum was remodelled as a fort by Aurelian, when he was building the circle of city walls. During medieval times, the castle became the Papal stronghold and prison, where many political opponents were tortured. During the time of the Borgias, a passageway was built to link the Vatican with the fortress. Inside there is a Papal suite and a military museum. The terrace gives an excellent panorama of St Peter's and the city of Rome. For opera buffs, the final scene of Puccini's *Tosca* was inspired by this terrace. The large bell was rung only to signal an execution.

The bronze angel perched on the castle pinnacle recalls a legend from about 600 AD, when an angel appeared to the Pope, heralding the end of a devastating plague. Hence the castle was renamed Sant'-Angelo. The castle became State property in 1870.
Open: 9-13 hrs. Entry 8,000 lire.

Aurelian Walls

A 12-mile ring of fortifications around the city, built during the reign of Emperor Aurelian (270-275 AD). Much of the wall still exists, in good condition. Several of the original eighteen main gates provide good vantage points from which to view the city, including Porta Pia (renovated by Michelangelo) and Porta San Paolo.

Augustus' Altar of Peace – Ara Pacis

Lungotevere in Augusta, near the Cavour Bridge on Via Ripetta

The reconstruction of a monumental altar erected by Augustus in 13 BC to celebrate the establishment of peace throughout the Roman lands, and the end of 20 years of civil war.
Open: Weekdays except Mon 9-19 hrs; Sun 9-13.45 hrs. Entrance 3,750 lire.

Chapter Five
Christian Rome

5.1 The historical setting

After the collapse of Imperial Rome, the city was effectively saved by the Papacy, which rose to strength amid the ruins. Political authority was vested in the bishops of Rome, who claimed prime status among western bishops, on the basis that the original Holy See had been founded by the Apostles Peter and Paul.

A federation of Papal States was established in 754, with Rome as the capital. Medieval Rome saw the building of churches, palaces and fortifications that used the monuments of classical Rome as a handy stone quarry.

There were long centuries of power struggles throughout the Middle Ages – between leading families, secular rulers and the popes.

During the 14th century – in 1309 – a French Pope Clement V moved the papal seat to Avignon in France.

However, by 1417 the papal court had moved permanently back to Rome, to revive the city as a place of pilgrimage.

During the Renaissance, the city flourished as never before, enjoying a key role when Italy became the cultural centre of the Western world. Under papal guidance there was a great wave of magnificent new building, briefly interrupted by the burning and looting of the city by German and Spanish troops in 1527.

Power struggles still continued, but the style of present-day Christian Rome was firmly established during those crucial centuries of the Renaissance.

CHRISTIAN ROME

5.2 *Vatican City*

Cross the line of white stones into St Peter's Square
and you leave Italy, to enter the completely independent Vatican State. This comprises Vatican City
itself – St Peter's, the Vatican palace, museums and
gardens, enclosed by fortress walls – and some
scattered properties such as four basilicas, several
seminaries, and the Pope's summer retreat at Castel
Gandolfo southeast of Rome.

Within the Vatican State's 109 acres are the Papal administrative offices, a radio station broadcast-
ing in around 30 languages, editorial offices for
varied periodicals and a daily Italian-language newspaper *L'Osservatore Romano*, a railway station,
helicopter pad and a postal service. Vatican postage
stamps are valid for correspondence posted throughout Rome. If you want a Vatican postmark, buy
stamps at the Post Office (left side of St Peter's
Square) and drop your letters or cards into the Vatican City's blue postboxes.

About a thousand people live in Vatican City,
including ninety members of the Swiss Guard,
dressed in traditional colours of the Medici Popes –
yellow, red and blue. Few of the Rome-based cardinals and bishops live within the Vatican City
walls, but they have the right to Vatican passports.

The best view of St Peter's is from the broad
approach-road called Via della Conciliazione, en-
abling one to appreciate the majestic dome,
designed by Michelangelo. On St Peter's Square
itself, you cannot see the full grandeur of the dome,
which reveals its full glory only from a distance.

St Peter's Square
An elliptical-shaped piazza designed by Bernini in
mid-17th century, enclosed by a great colonnade.
When the Pope is in residence, he appears on his
balcony (top floor, second window from right) at 12
noon Sunday and pronounces a Papal blessing on
the crowds gathered around the Egyptian obelisk in
the Piazza below. Greatest of these occasions is on
Easter Sunday when a million worshippers crowd

the Square for the traditional Easter blessing –
"Urbi et Orbi" – to the City and the World.

The central obelisk, incidentally, 'witnessed' the
martyrdom of St Peter. Brought by Roman conquerors from Heliopolis in Egypt, it stood originally in
Nero's Circus Vaticanus where the apostle was
crucified. In an oft-repeated story, the obelisk was
re-erected in St Peter's Square in 1586. The task of
setting up the obelisk had almost failed because the
ropes were too taut to take the final strain. A
sailor's cry "Water on the ropes!" saved the situa-
tion.

St Peter's Basilica

Open: 7-19 hrs. Entrance free.

First built as a shrine in 324 AD for the mortal
remains of St Peter, the Basilica was rebuilt over a
thousand years later. Various architects and artists
worked on the building, including Bramante, Raphael, Michelangelo and Peruzzi. Finally completed
in the shape of a Latin Cross, St Peter's in its present form was consecrated in 1626.

Immediately right after you enter is Michelangelo's most famous work, the Pietà, sculpted when
he was 25 years' old and already at the height of
his creative genius. The masterpiece has been pro-
tected by bulletproof glass ever since 1972 when a
crazed Hungarian attacked the sculpture with a
hammer.

On the floor of the central nave are marked the
lengths of other well-known cathedrals. All are
dwarfed by St Peter's. St Paul's, London, comes
closest, falling short by 102 feet.

On the right, as you approach the Papal altar, is
a bronze statue of St Peter, whose right foot is now
worn smooth after being kissed by millions of pilgrims ever since the 13th century.

The Papal altar was designed by Bernini, and is
known as the Baldacchino (a baldaquin or canopy).
Bees carved on the columns are the emblem of the
Barbarini family, to which Urban VIII belonged
when he unveiled the canopy in 1633. In front of
the altar, on a lower level, is the reputed tomb of
St Peter, centred beneath the awe-inspiring dome.

CHRISTIAN ROME

St Peter's Chair

At the furthest end of the apse is a bronze monument by Bernini, made in 1665 to encase the wooden chair in which St Peter reputedly sat when making his first sermons in Rome.

To the right is a Baroque tomb, also by Bernini, purpose built for Pope Urban VIII who commissioned his own memorial in 1628, sixteen years before he died.

St Peter's Treasury, inside St Peter's

A modern, well displayed museum giving a chance to see many treasures and past glories: chalices, crosses, vestments and early Christian relics.
Open 9-18.30 hrs. Entrance 3,000 lire.

View from the top

To appreciate Michelangelo's dome, what better way than by climbing to the top! This is possible every day from 8-18 hrs.

Outside the Basilica, to the right, is entrance to the lift which carries you to the 18-ft-high statues that overlook the square – a good viewpoint for photographs and a cup of coffee. Inside the dome, you also get a close-up view of the superb mosaics.

The top of the dome is then accessible by climbing some 300 stairs up a narrow spiral. If you can make it to the exterior gallery, the reward is a spectacular view right across Rome.

A visit to the Dome costs 6,000 lire by lift, or 5,000 lire by stairs.

Papal Audience

With a letter from your priest, you can get admission tickets from the Prefectura's office which is open Monday and Tuesday mornings. For information, Tel: 6982.

Travel agencies can also make arrangements. General Papal audiences take place Wednesday mornings in the 7,000-seat Aula Paolo VI auditorium from 10-12 hrs when the Pope is in Rome; otherwise, on Sundays during July and August, at the Pope's summer residence at Castel Gandolfo in the Alban Hills outside Rome.

5.3 The Vatican Museums

The entrance is located in Viale Vaticano, reached by a brisk walk outside the Vatican walls to the north side of Vatican City, 300 yards from Piazza del Risorgimento. The nearest Metro station is Ottaviano.

Admission price is 15,000 lire, which includes all sections of the main museum, the Sistine Chapel, the Pinacoteca, the Missionary-Ethnological Museum and the Carriage Museum.

The museums are open daily Mon-Sat 8.45-13.00 hrs. During April to mid-June, and in Sep-Oct, open until 16 hrs except for a Sat closing time of 13 hrs.

On the last Sunday of each month, the museums are open from 8.45-13 hrs, with free entrance. The Vatican Museums are closed on all other Sundays and religious holidays.

The collections are housed in 1000 rooms and corridors. Needless to say, it would take a lifetime to see everything in detail! Short-stay visitors often skim through in 90 minutes, with a short pause at selected highlights.

Devotees should assign at least a whole day, perhaps following a recommended routing that takes five hours to complete. There's a snack bar for restoring the exhausted.

If you want a compromise between those two extremes, take an organised tour with a guide who can bring those highlights vividly to life. For guide-yourself visitors, headphones can be rented for the Sistine Chapel and the Raphael Rooms. Remember to have 100- or 200-lire coins handy.

At the entrance, you take a lift to an upper floor and work down to ground level. Routing is on a one-way system, so you cannot backtrack. There is a colour-coded choice of four different routes including an Egyptian Museum, the Pio Clementino Museum of Greek and Roman antiquities, varied galleries and of course the Sistine Chapel.

Some routes pause for the Vatican Library, containing many treasures including love letters from Henry VIII to Anne Boleyn.

CHRISTIAN ROME

Sistine Chapel

The Sistine Chapel, named after Pope Sixtus IV, is the Pope's private chapel where the cardinals meet when it's time to elect a new pope.

Built at the end of the 15th century, it was decorated by some of history's greatest artists, including Botticelli, Perugino and Ghirlandaio, who painted the side walls.

But the chapel is best known for the contribution of Michelangelo. Commissioned to paint the ceiling in 1508 by Pope Julius II, he completed it within four years, working single-handed while lying on his back. Some twenty years later he was asked to paint the altar wall, *The Last Judgement*, regarded as one of the greatest masterpieces of Renaissance art.

In 1984 the immense ten-year task began of restoring Michelangelo's ceiling paintings – dedicated work by three Italian specialists who employed the same historic design of scaffolding used by Michelangelo himself.

The work was financed by a $3 million gift from a Japanese TV company in exchange for all filming, book and photographic rights until the beginning of the 21st century.

The ceiling portrays the main events from the Book of Genesis: God separates light and darkness; creates sun, moon and plant life; divides land and sea; creates Adam and Eve; then the Fall, and Expulsion from Eden; Noah's Sacrifice, followed by the Flood, and Noah's Drunkenness.

Results of the ceiling restoration have been truly magnificent, revealing every detail in the original brilliance of colour. Luminosity has been restored to scenes that had been darkened by centuries of candle smoke. Judge for yourself! Take binoculars or opera glasses, to intensify your enjoyment.

The end wall, devoted to *The Last Judgement*, has awed millions of visitors since Michelangelo painted the huge composition of nearly three hundred figures, the elect and the damned, with a stern Jesus standing beardless in the centre.

The newly restored painting has been revealed in its full glory to the public since April 1994.

The Borgia Apartment

In the year that Columbus sailed to the New World, 1492, the Borgia Pope Alexander VI commissioned frescoes by Pinturicchio as decoration for the 6-room living quarters used by the Popes for the following hundred years. The frescoes have recently been restored.

Room IV was used by Alexander as his study. The Pope's daughter Lucrezia posed for the portrait of St Catherine in the next room.

The Borgia Apartment now forms part of a 55-room group that houses a collection of **Modern Religious Art**, inaugurated by Pope Paul VI in 1973. Among the eight hundred paintings are works by Francis Bacon, Munch, Kokoschka, Chagall and Picasso.

The Raphael Rooms (Stanze di Raffaello)

In 1508 Pope Julius II took a dislike to the existing decorations in these private apartments, and sent for 26-year-old Raphael – then living in Florence – to take on the assignment.

In the first room is a Perugino ceiling, with the *Fire of Borgo* painting designed by Raphael, illustrating a great fire of 847 which was extinguished when Pope Leo IV made the Sign of the Cross.

In the next room, the Stanza della Segnatura, are Raphael's two major frescoes – *Disputation on the Holy Sacrament* and the *School of Athens*. The latter painting symbolizes the Renaissance itself, with its new respect for the philosophy of classical Greece.

The final room in the apartment was painted by pupils and assistants after Raphael's early death in 1520, but following the designs he had already prepared.

Vatican Picture Gallery – the Pinacoteca

The gallery's eighteen rooms display a fabulous collection of paintings from the 11th to the 19th centuries, all arranged in chronological order. It includes some of the world's greatest masterpieces that comprise a virtual history of Italian art from the Byzantine style to the finest works of the Renaissance.

CHRISTIAN ROME

There are treasures by Giotto, Fra Angelico, Filippo Lippi, Raphael (including the *Coronation of the Virgin*, painted when he was 20), Caravaggio, Titian and Leonardo de Vinci. Ten tapestries designed by Raphael for hanging in the Sistine Chapel are also displayed here.

Museo Storico – Historical Museum
This contains carriages, arms, uniforms and relics of the disbanded Papal armies.

Vatican Gardens
These beautifully kept gardens can be visited every day except Wed, March to the end of October.

Guided tours start from the Information Office at 10 a.m. Cost: 18,000 lire, with advance booking. The office is on the left-hand side of St Peter's Square, near the Arco delle Campane (the Bell Arch). For information, tel: 69884466 or 69884866.

5.4 The Catacombs

There are many to explore: 120 miles of catacombs, compared with only 25 miles of Metro. If time is limited, choose the Catacombs of S. Agnese, close to the centre of Rome on the Via Nomentana. Otherwise, if more time is available, go out along the Appian Way – so rich in early Christian history. A pilgrimage through the long burial chambers is a memorable experience. The simplest tombs were dug and shaped into cubicles or crypts to hold sarcophagi. Among the best known are:

Catacombe di San Sebastiano
Via Appia Antica 132, beneath the church of San Sebastiano

This is prime choice. Three mausoleums with stucco decorations date from the 1st century. It is believed that the bodies of Saints Peter and Paul were concealed here until their permanent basilicas were built.
Open: Daily 8.30-12.00 & 14.30-17.00 hrs. Closed Thu, and from mid-Jan to mid-Feb. Entrance: 8,000 lire.   Tel: 7887035

Catacombe di San Callisto

Via Appia Antica 110 – just along the road from San Sebastiano.

Built on four levels, as the first official Christian burial place in Rome, and extending several kilometres. The complex dates from the 2nd century, with innumerable 3rd, 7th and 8th century frescoes. This was also the 3rd century crypt of the popes.
Open: Daily 8.30-12 & 14.30-17.30 hrs. Closed Wed and in Feb. Entry: 8,000 lire. Tel: 5136725

Domine Quo Vadis? (1637 AD)

Along the same Appian Way as the catacombs mentioned above, this small church marks the reputed setting for the legend that when St Peter was fleeing from persecution in Rome, he was met by an image of Jesus. Peter asked "Quo vadis, domine?" – "Whither goest thou, lord?" Christ replied "I am going to Rome, to be crucified again."

Shamed, Peter turned back to Rome, was crucified upside down in Nero's circus, and buried under Vatican Hill.

Catacombe di Priscilla   Tel: 86206272

Via Salaria 430, on the northern side of Rome.

These catacombs contain 2nd century frescoes. Amongst them is the oldest known image of the Madonna and Child.
Open: 8.30-12.00 & 14.30-17.00 hrs. Closed Mon. Entrance: 8,000 lire.

5.5 The major churches

Rome is a city of 300 churches, of which 80 are dedicated to the Virgin Mary. Here's a short list of the most interesting.

St Mary Major (Santa Maria Maggiore)

Metro: Cavour or Termini

This basilica is the largest of the churches dedicated to Mary. Built by Pope Sixtus III (432-440), with an 18th-century facade and the tallest campanile in Rome from 1380. This splendid medieval

monument contains some 36 panels of beautiful mosaics. The Old Testament scenes are well worth studying. At the end of the nave, a triumphal arch is decorated with scenes of the Annunciation, and the childhood of Christ including Our Lady. Other treasures include the Pauline Chapel.
Open: 7-19 hrs.

St Laurence outside the walls
(San Lorenzo fuori le mura) Piazzale del Verano

An intriguing church, originally the site of a chapel built in the 4th century by Constantine the Great over the tomb of St Lawrence, martyred by being grilled over a gridiron. By the Middle Ages two churches had been built back to back, which were later joined to form one. If you ask at the Sacristy, you may be able to see the 12th century double cloisters. A tip is in order here.
Open: April-Sept 9-18.30; Oct-Mar 9-14.30 hrs.

St John Lateran (San Giovanni in Laterano)
Metro: San Giovanni (Line A)

Founded in 313 AD during the reign of Constantine the Great, St John Lateran was the cathedral of Rome for about 1000 years, and Papal coronations were held here until the 19th century.

The central bronze gate with its two porticos came from the ancient Curia in the Forum. There are many beautiful mosaics to see, and a restored fresco by Giotto in the middle nave.

The basilica is perhaps best known for its 'Scala Santa' – Holy Staircase. According to tradition, the 28 marble stairs were originally in Pilate's residence in Jerusalem, and were used by Christ during his trial. The steps are still climbed by pilgrims on their knees.
Open: 7.00-18.30 hrs, but some parts (such as the Scala Santa) are closed 12.30-15.30 hrs. Be sure to visit the 13th-century cloisters!

Chapter Six

Baroque to 20th century

6.1 Historical update

During the 17th century, Rome saw another great period of building and expansion, with Baroque style in the ascendant.

The first major architect in this exuberant style was Carlo Maderno, who worked on St Peter's and who was initially responsible for the Barberini Palace which is now the National Gallery of Ancient Art.

The early works of Francesco Borromini took the new style a step further, particularly with his 1638 design of S. Carlo alle Quattro Fontane on Via del Quirinale.

But it was Bernini who set the pace, designing churches and especially creating highly imaginative fountains which had such influence on the style and appearance of Rome today.

The transformation of the Piazza Navona became a trend-setter for later civic landmarks such as the 18th-century Spanish Steps and the Trevi Fountain. Squares and fountains became an essential part of city design, even late into the 19th century.

Meanwhile, in late 18th and early 19th centuries, a reaction came to the more florid aspects of Baroque and Rococo, and the Neo-Classic style marked some return to the simplicity of ancient Greece and Rome.

The Napoleonic Wars brought a temporary setback to the city, with quantities of art treasures carried off to France. Napoleon annexed the Papal States, which were all returned to the Vatican in 1814; but not the works of art.

BAROQUE ROME

Unification of Italy

In 1849, the charismatic leader, Garibaldi, began the *Risorgimento* which led to the final unification of Italy in 1870. Rome became the capital of a united Italy under King Victor Emmanuel II, whose white-marble monument overlooks Piazza Venezia, the roaring traffic hub of central Rome. To make room for the so-called 'white typewriter', rows of medieval houses were removed from the slopes of the Capitoline Hill. New streets were laid out, such as Via Nazionale to link Piazza Venezia to Piazza Esedra and the main railway station.

In 1922 Mussolini marched on Rome, and established Fascist government. In 1929 the Lateran Pact gave independent and sovereign status to Vatican City. The Great Dictator, ensconced in the Palazzo Venezia, dreamed of restoring Italy to the grandeur of Imperial Rome. In 1932, so that he could look direct from his balcony to the Colosseum, Mussolini decreed the bulldozing of one of Rome's oldest medieval quarters. The 930-yard highway, 88 yards wide, was named Via dell'Impero – today's Via dei Fori Imperiali – which would be suitable for triumphant military parades.

The declaration of Rome as an Open City during World War II was effective in saving the city from further damage. In 1946 Italy again became a Republic.

6.2 A selection of Roman delights

The Spanish Steps (1726)

Much of the colour of Rome is supplied by the visitors themselves. At the Spanish Steps, tourists by the thousand, dressed in all kinds of gear, provide a huge source of entertainment to the local Roman youth. During the March-April Spring Festival, the Steps are covered in massed flowers. Then, at least until October, the Spanish Steps are covered in tourists, even more sun-ripened pink than the April azaleas.

It's like a setting for open-air opera, with a large and brilliant chorus ready to break out any moment into song, dance or drama. Young backpackers sit writing letters home. Others just sit, waiting for something to happen, and meanwhile enjoying the passing scene.

Occasional groups burst into song, especially if someone has brought a guitar. Tourists take photos of artists' drawing caricatures of tourists taking photographs. Some of the more decorative off-duty soldiers of the Italian Army parade their uniforms in front of female tourists, and look eager.

To the tinkle of horse-bells, carriages wait hopefully in the Piazza di Spagna for the perfect tourist who may take a 50-minute ride without asking the price first.

Altogether, it's a fun place to visit. The sightseeing rationale is the splendid view over to St Peter's, seen from the top terrace where the church of Trinità dei Monti dominates the skyline. The boat-shaped fountain in the square was designed by Bernini's father, Pietro. The sculpture of a stranded boat, leaking badly, is called 'Fontana della Barcaccia' and is used by many sightseers to bathe their aching feet. Directly opposite is Via Condotti, the city's most expensive shopping street.

Keats-Shelley Memorial House
Piazza di Spagna   Tel: 6784235
A little corner of England, beside the Spanish Steps: the house where Keats died in 1821, preserved as a memorial to the Romantic poets. The floor where Keats lived is filled to the brim with pictures, letters and mementoes of Keats, Shelley, Byron and Leigh Hunt. Everything is labelled in English and Italian. Just opposite is Babington's Tea Room, offering high-priced English tea and muffins. Open: Mon-Fri 9-13 & 15-18 hrs. Entry 5,000 lire.

Trevi Fountain
The Trevi Fountain starred in the movie *Three Coins in the Fountain*, and has never since lacked publicity. It's one of Rome's liveliest corners, with souvenir vendors, stalls selling hot pizza, hundreds of tourists throwing coins into the fountain, or posing for cameras against the Trevi background.

BAROQUE ROME

Cleaning up

An average $300 a day is cast into the spectacular cascade of water and marble, under the benevolent gaze of Neptune with a supporting cast of Salubrity and Abundance, four statues that depict the seasons, and tritons riding sea-horses. Who goes fishing? The coinage harvest is devoted to charities, including the International Red Cross. A private enterprise team once started cleaning up at night: they ended in gaol instead.

Piazza Navona

A very charming and popular square, especially in the evening, full of vendors' selling paintings, sketches and jewellery. After a hard day's sightseeing, here's a great place to rest your weary feet. In ancient times, the area was covered by a large stadium or circus built by Domitian (81-96 AD) – hence the elliptical shape.

After falling into disuse, the area was revived in the 15th century, and remains one of the most delightful pedestrian areas in Rome. If you're in Rome during the Christmas and New Year period, visit the Piazza for its traditional Christmas Market running from 15 December to 6 January.

Particularly the Piazza Navona is known for its fountains:

La Fontana dei Quattro Fiume – The Fountain of Four Rivers, designed by Gian Lorenzo Bernini and representing the Ganges, Nile, Danube and Plate Rivers. Magnificent!

Fontana del Moro – Fountain of the Moor. The fountain was built in late 16th century. The main character, the Moor, was designed by Bernini in 1653 when he was commissioned to renovate the monument.

Fontana di Nettuno – Neptune's Fountain was likewise constructed in 16th century, but Neptune and the surrounding figures were not installed until the 19th century.

Chapter Seven

Museums and Galleries

7.1 Opening hours

Rome offers four types of Museum: – State – Municipal – Vatican – Private.

The state museums, galleries and monuments can usually be visited free of charge on the first and third Saturday, and on the second and fourth Sunday of the month. They also offer free admission (show passport) to British citizens under 18 or over 60. They include Castel Sant'Angelo, the Etruscan Museum at Villa Giulia, National Roman Museum, National Gallery in the Palazzo Barberini, the Museum of Oriental Art and the Modern Art Museum.

Municipal museums and galleries (for example, Capitoline and Barracco Museums) and the Vatican Museums are free on the last Sunday of the month.

Times of opening are liable to change at a moment's notice! So be prepared.

Staff problems or renovations can disrupt opening times, or close off entire sections of great museums, sometimes for months or years on end. Most museums close one day a week, usually either on Monday or Tuesday. Before making a special journey across Rome, check the current opening hours from listings held by the hotel concierge.

Caution: on the principal public holidays, virtually all shops, museums and galleries are closed. The compensation is that central Rome is then a paradise for pedestrians.

Entrance fees range from about 6,000 to 18,000 lire. These fees are also liable to change, but the figures listed will at least give an indication of the price level to expect.

7.2 A museum short-list

Capitoline Museums – Musei Capitolini
Piazza dei Campidoglio (near Piazza Venezia)

The twin-palace Capitoline Museums house Europe's oldest public art collection, founded 1471 by Pope Sixtus IV who needed space for his accumulation of Greek and Roman sculptures. The Piazza itself was designed by Michelangelo in 1538, but was not completed until a hundred years later.

In the Palace – likewise designed by Michelangelo – the most renowned works are the *Capitoline Venus*, the *Dying Gaul* and the well-known sculpture by Pellaiolo of the Etruscan wolf nursing Romulus and Remus.

Among the rich collection of paintings are works by Titian, Rubens and Caravaggio.

Open: 9-19 hrs. Mon closed. Sun 9-13.45 hrs.
Entrance 10,000 lire.   Tel: 67102071

Roman Civilization Museum
Museo della Civiltà Romana – Piazza G. Agnelli
Metro – Line B to EUR – Stop: Fermi.

Special for history buffs: reproductions which document Roman history, and the expansion of the Empire. Of particular interest is the scale model of ancient Rome. This museum was built by the Fiat company, and donated to the city.

Open: 9-19 hrs. Mon closed. Sun 9-13 hrs.
Entrance 5,000 lire.   Tel: 5926135

Etruscan Museum – Villa Giulia
Piazza Villa Giulia, in the north-west corner of
Borghese Gardens   Tel: 3201951

Built as a villa in mid-16th century by pleasure-loving Pope Julius III, this magnificent Renaissance building contains the world's finest collection of Etruscan art and artifacts from pre-Roman times. Highlights include the recumbent *Sarcophagus of the Married Couple* in terracotta, from 6th century BC; the *Apollo of Veio* sculpture; and innumerable finds from Etruscan cemeteries, well laid out.

Open: 9-19 hrs. Mon closed. Entrance 8,000 lire.

Museum of Palazzo Venezia

Piazza Venezia   Tel: 6798865

Splendidly located at Rome's busiest traffic intersection, the Venezia Palace was built mid-15th century, and later given to the Venetian Republic for use as their embassy – hence the name. The building was frequently seen on news-reels of the 1930's, when dictator Mussolini made impassioned speeches from the central balcony to cheering crowds in the piazza below. From that balcony Mussolini declared war against Britain and France on 10 June 1940, just after Dunkirk, when he felt the time was ripe to help Hitler divide the spoils of victory.

Today the palace houses a collection of paintings, statues, tapestries and porcelains, supplemented by temporary art exhibitions. Most interesting is the Map Room (Sala del Mappamondo) – so named for its wall painting of the world as depicted in 1495. This enormous room – 70 feet by 40 – was used by Mussolini as his single-occupancy office.

Open: Tues-Sat 9-14; Sun and holidays 9-13 hrs; Mon closed. Entrance 8,000 lire.

National Roman Museum – Museo delle Terme

Entrance Piazza della Repubblica / Piazza dei Cinquecento, across the square from Termini Station   Tel: 4880856

More of the glory of ancient Rome – the Baths of Diocletian, built 298 AD. It was largest of all the Roman Baths, 32 acres in area, even bigger than the Caracalla complex.

The water supply was cut off in 538 AD, and the Baths fell into disuse. Today, part of the site is devoted to the National Roman Museum which houses a great collection of Greek and Roman statues, and beautiful mosaics.

A masterpiece of 1st-century Classical art is the fresco that covered four walls from a room in the Empress Livia's villa at Prima Porta, north of Rome. Its vivid colours make it hard to believe it was painted almost 2000 years ago!

Open: Tues–Sat 9-14; Sun 9-13 hrs; Mon closed. Entrance: 12,000 lire.

MUSEUMS

Galleria Barberini (Palazzo Barberini)

Via Quattro Fontane. Metro: Barberini.

A Baroque palace built by Cardinal Maffeo Barberini after he became Pope Urban VIII. The architects were the two top men of Baroque style – Borromini and Bernini, who worked on this spectacular Barberini family home from 1627 to 1633. On the Piazza Barberini is the delightful **Fountain of the Bees**, also by Bernini. Bees were the emblem of the Barberini family.

Today, the huge building is occupied partly by Italy's National Gallery, and partly by a military organisation. One of the gems of the collection is Raphael's portrait of his bosomy mistress, *La Fornarina*. There is also a portrait of Henry VIII by Holbein; and works by El Greco, Titian, Guardi, Canaletto and Lippi.

The apartments of the Barberini family are worth visiting for their costumes, china and period furniture.

Open: 9-19 hrs. Sun 9-13 hrs. Closed Mon.
Entrance: 8,000 lire.   Tel: 4814591

Galleria Borghese

Piazzale del Museo Borghese   Tel: 8548577

A relatively small palace, built 1613 for the wealthy Cardinal Scipione Borghese – Pope Paul V – who was a great collector of ancient statues. In 1803 Prince Camillo Borghese married Napoleon's sister, Pauline, and most of the original collection was shipped to the Louvre in Paris.

The present sculpture collection was formed after Camillo's death, and is displayed on the ground floor. The most renowned work is a statue of Pauline Bonaparte, carved by Canova. Pauline enjoyed a lively reputation in Rome – especially while her husband was away supervizing his estates in Northern Italy – and displays herself nude, as Venus the goddess of love.

The upper floor of the Borghese Gallery has been closed lengthily for restoration, and re-opening remains vague. Paintings by Raphael, Caravagggio and others are meanwhile displayed in the Complesso Monumentale at Via di San Michele 22 in

The Spanish Steps, finished in 1726, have long been the place to be seen.

Across the Tiber to the Vatican.

The Colosseum, scene of gladiatorial combat between condemed men and exotic wildlife.

A Swiss Guard on duty in Vatican City.

Statue of St Peter the apostle, who spent many years in Rome before he was crucified in AD67.

St Peter's towers above the River Tiber.

Rome is dotted with fountains and obelsiks. Each stands as a reminder of the city's glorious past.

Trastevere.
Open: Tues-Sat 9-19; Sun & Hols 9-13 hrs.
Entrance 4,000 lire.

Galleria Colonna, Via della Pilotta 17

A private collection housed in the huge Palazzo Colonna (another of Rome's great families). Specials include a Veronese portrait of an unknown nobleman, a set of landscapes by Gaspare Dughet, and paintings by Tintoretto and Poussin.
Open Saturdays only, 9-13 hrs. Closed in August.
Entrance: 10,000 lire.   Tel: 6794362

Galleria Doria Pamphili

Piazza del Collegio Romano 1a
  A small gallery bursting at the seams with gems, including a Velasquez portrait of Pope Innocento X, a member of the Pamphili family. Other masterpieces include works by Rubens, Filippo Lippi, Caravaggio and Breughel. An easy-to-manage gallery! It is advisable to buy the catalogue, as the pictures only have numbers on them.
  The entrance fee includes the picture gallery only, and there is a supplement of 5,000 lire for the State apartments. These are a 'must'. Visitors are guided by a curator, and a tip is recommended.
Open: Mon, Tue, Fri, Sat & Sun 10-13 hrs.
Entrance: 10,000 lire.   Tel: 6797323

Galleria Nazional d'Arte Moderna

Viale delle Belle Arti 131   Tel: 3224152
  The National Gallery of Modern Art features the 19th and 20th centuries, including works by Matisse, Picasso and Modigliani.
Open: Tue-Sat 9-19 hrs; Sun & Hols 9-13 hrs.
Entrance: 8,000 lire.

Chapter Eight

Go shopping

8.1 The markets

During early classical times, the Roman Forum was the city-centre trading area. Then, from 2nd century BC onwards, as the central location was increasingly devoted to public monuments, specialized markets were located along the Tiber – one for meat, another for fruit and vegetables, a third for fish. Shops in the central area were devoted to the sale of luxury goods such as pearls, precious stones and antiques.

Rome's first major multi-storey shopping centre was Trajan's Market, built in early 2nd century AD on the slopes of the Quirinal Hill. The brick construction on five floors could accommodate 150 shops. The slopes of the Capitoline Hill were also used as a lively marketplace which continued to operate until the 15th century, when the activities were transferred to Piazza Navona.

Campo de'Fiori

The Piazza Navona market stayed until 1869, when it was relocated to the present-day Campo de'Fiori – close to the river, a few blocks north of Ponte Sisto bridge. This piazza had already been well established during the 15th century as a craft centre, but also doubled as a place of execution for heretics. The central statue is dedicated to Giordano Bruno, a monk who was burned for heresy in 1600, during the period of the Counter-Reformation.

Street names around the piazza reflect the original craft activities, such as Via dei Cappellari for the hat-makers and Via dei Baullari for the trunk-makers. The extra trading influx from 1869 converted Campo de'Fiori into the most important market in the city, where just about everything could be bought and sold.

From 1948, elements of the old market were moved to other locations, leaving the piazza as a colourful neighbourhood food market. It's full of character, giving you a chance to hear Italian at its most colloquial. Open Mon-Sat 6 a.m. until 2 p.m.

Porta Portese Flea Market
In the Trastevere area, close to Ponte Sublicio, this Sunday-morning flea market from around Porta Portese and along the Via Portuense offers a lively atmosphere. You can buy almost anything from junk antiques to new and used clothing. Always barter! There are few real bargains, but it's all good-humoured fun. Because of the crowds, be extra careful with purses and wallets.

Via Sannio Clothes Market
This is Rome's biggest open-air clothing market, to the side of Porta San Giovanni, along a stretch of the ancient Roman wall.
Open Mon-Sat until 1 p.m.
Metro San Giovanni (Linea A); or bus no 4, 81, 85 or 87.

Via Trionfale Flower Market
Located north of Vatican City at 47/49 Via Trionfale, this two-level produce hall covers Italy's third largest wholesale cut-flower market. It is strictly reserved for dealers only, except on Tuesdays when the public is admitted from 10 a.m. until 1 p.m. to look around and buy retail.

The Antiques Market
When the Campo de'Fiori market was reorganised in 1948, the antiques sector found a permanent site at Piazza Fontanella Borghese (near the River, in a direct line from Via Condotti). It's a happy hunting ground for collectors of Roman coins, silver pieces, second-hand books, musical scores, old maps, prints and engravings. Open weekdays 9-19 hrs.

SHOPPING

Piazza Vittorio Emanuele

Reached by Metro – Line A to Vittorio Emanuele –
or close to Santa Maria Maggiore if you're walking, this is Rome's largest and most colourful market, spread around a huge garden piazza. There's
every variety of food stall on the north side, and
leather and clothing on the south.

8.2 Shops and department stores

All shops are tightly shuttered and streets empty for
lunch and siesta, from 12.30 or 1 p.m. till 3.30 or
4 p.m. Then business continues till 7.30 or 8.
Shops are open Monday to Saturday, mostly with
Saturday afternoon closed. In winter, shops don't
bother to open Monday morning.

Opposite the Spanish Steps is Via Condotti,
where wealthy Romans go shopping. Italian men
say: "It's heaven for ladies, but hell for husbands."

For Italy's finest displays of jewellery, just pre-
tend to be a millionaire and stroll through the
breathtaking showrooms of Bulgari – just a few
steps down Via Condotti, and considered to be one
of the world's greatest jewelry shops.

Along the Via Condotti, fragrant with big names
like Gucci, most of the goods displayed are not
priced; or the figures are so discreet that you need
binoculars to read them. If you have to know the
price before deciding to buy, you can't afford it!
There are shirts at £80, shoes that start at £100,
while a simple trouser belt costs £40.

The parallel and side streets are likewise into the
jewellery and high-fashion business. At the cheaper
end of the area, shoes sink as low as £50 a pair.

Here are some more high-fashion shopping areas,
and the designer labels to look for:

Via Borgognona: Gianfranco Ferre; Fendi; Given-
chy.

Via del Babuino: Giorgio Armani; Gente; Kenzo;
Missoni.

Via Bocca de Leone: Valentino; Trussardi Gianni
Versace; Ungaro; Yves St Laurent and other French
designers like Courrèges, Balenciaga and Céline.

Department stores

La Rinascente – Piazza Colonna and Piazza Fiume

Upim – has 18 branches with products at moderate prices. Via del Tritone 172 is the most central branch.

Standa – Via Cola di Rienzo 173 is the most central branch of the chain.

Prima – Via Nazionale 252, claims to be Rome's largest department store.

Best buys

To local Romans on average incomes, best value shopping can be found in the Via Cola di Rienzo area, near the Vatican (metro: Ottaviano). Other middle income citizens choose the stores of Via Nazionale or Via del Corso. Sometimes bargains can be found in the Trevi Fountain district.

8.3 Clothing Sizes

There is no exact science about conversions between British, North American and Italian clothing sizes. The following figures offer some rough guidance as a prelude to trying on garments before purchase.

Women's dresses and suits

British	32	34	36	38	40	42
or British	6	8	10	12	14	16
USA	4	6	8	10	12	14
Italian	38	40	42	44	46	48

Men's suits and coats

UK & USA	36	38	40	42	44	46
Italian	46	48	50	52	54	56

Men's Shirts

UK & USA	14½	15	15½	16	16½	17
Italian	37	38	39	40	42	43

Women's Shoes

UK	2	3	4	5	6	7	8
USA	3	4	5	6	7	8	9
Italian	34	36	37	38	39	40	41

Men's Shoes

UK	5	6	7	8	9	10	11
USA	6	7	8	9	10	11	12
Italian	38	39	41	42	43	44	46

8.4 Weights and measures

Unless you want pocket calculator accuracy, here are some quick conversions which are good enough for most purposes.

Length

1 inch = 2.54 or 2½ centimetres
1 foot = .3 metres
1 mile = 1.6 kilometres; or multiply by 8, divide by 5
1 centimetre = 0.40 or 2/5ths inches
1 metre = 3.3 feet
1 kilometre = 0.62 miles; or multiply by 5, divide by 8

Weight

1 ounce = 30 grammes
1 pound = 0.45 kilogrammes; just under half a kilo
1 kilo = 2.2 or 2 1/5th pounds
1 gramme = 1/30 ounce

Fluid

1 Imperial pint = 0.6 or 3/5ths litres
1 US pint = half a litre
1 litre = 1.75 Imperial pints; or 2 US pints.

Chapter Nine
Take a trip

Of course, no city break is long enough for all the sightseeing that Rome can offer. But, for a change of scene, why not take a trip out of town? There are many possibilities. But let's keep the short-list down to a choice of two all-time favourites: half-day Tivoli and Villa d'Este; or whole-day Naples, Pompeii and Sorrento.

9.1 Tivoli and Villa d'Este

For a morning or afternoon outing, the most popular trip is to the hillside village of Tivoli, where wealthy Romans built their splendid summer palaces, 19 miles east of the city. En route, as the road climbs, you pass through centuries'-old olive groves. The old road also passes the sulphur baths of Bagni di Tivoli, but there's no need to halt unless you get high on sulphuretted hydrogen.

At Tivoli itself, the 16th-century fountains, cascades and gardens of the Villa d'Este are the principal attraction – a cool relief during the hot summer season. The entire 7-acre complex is refreshing and light-hearted, to comprise one of Europe's most delightful water fantasies.

Open: 9 a.m. until 1½ hours before sunset. Closed on some holidays.

Entrance 8,000 lire.   Tel: 0774-22070

Villa Adriana

Many Tivoli tours include a visit to the ruins of Hadrian's Villa, built 125-135 AD. There was nothing suburban about *this* villa! The 3-mile perimeter of the emperor's estate enclosed a mammoth project which included an imperial palace, several baths, a couple of theatres and some libraries.

Within this idyllic summer retreat, Hadrian reproduced many ideas of art and architecture which he had acquired during lengthy travels around the Roman Empire. Some 300 items from his collection of sculptures and other objets d'art now adorn the major museums of Europe.

Open: 9 a.m. until 1½ hours before sunset. Closed on some holidays.

Entrance 8,000 lire.   Tel: 0774-530203

9.2 Naples and Pompeii

A motorway southwards brings Naples, Pompeii and Sorrento within reach of a whole-day excursion. It's a long trail, but very rewarding: the final stage of the old-time Grand Tour which normally ended with a sojourn in Naples and an awed visit to the smoking lip of Mount Vesuvius.

Building of the Autostrada del Sole – the Sunshine Motorway – has eased the strain of doing the trip by road. But the overall day's mileage is still over 300. Do-it-yourself travellers, with more time to make their own way, could cover the Rome-Naples sector by one of the fast trains from Termini Station – 2 hours for the 134-mile journey.

Naples? On a quick drive round, you can get a good impression of the superbly beautiful Bay of Naples, especially when viewed from the up-market residential area called Vomero. Perhaps there's time to pause at Santa Lucia – the fishing harbour that launched the song – where the waterfront is lined with seafood restaurants. Otherwise, the joyous street life of central Naples is best seen from the armchair comfort of the motor coach.

Out past the industrial zone, otherwise lacking in sightseeing potential, you start getting good views of Vesuvius. Along the road is a richly fertile garden landscape, green with vineyards and lush vegetation. In that gorgeous setting, it's easy to understand why farmers have continued to work the terraced hillsides despite what happened in AD 79, when Vesuvius blew its top.

Cameo country

Pompeii is magnificent. Excavation continues. Every year there are more discoveries that help archaeologists reconstruct every tiny detail of daily life in the city that suddenly died nineteen centuries ago. Fascinating!

Along the highway from Naples are numerous workshops that specialise in manufacture of cameos, and it's possible to enter and watch the artists at work. Beware of cheap plastic imitations offered by street vendors!

Some day trips manage to include Sorrento – perched on a cliff-top, with a perpendicular drop to a very narrow strip of beach. Major first-class hotels are lined along the cliff amid luxuriant gardens, dripping with flowers everywhere. Views across the Bay are idyllic.

Time for shopping? Sorrento specialises in wood and mother-of-pearl inlaid work, leather items, hand-embroidered linen, silks, cameos, coral and onyx. Many items you can buy direct from side-street workshops.

Next time you're in Italy, consider combining Sorrento and Rome in a two-centre holiday. With an extra day, you could include the dreamy island of Capri with its Blue Grotto and Villa of San Michele: utterly delightful if you can avoid the overcrowded high season.

Chapter Ten
Learn Italian

Don't worry if you cannot speak Italian. In the main hotels, restaurants, bars and shops, service staff have at least a smattering of most West European languages. If not, there's always someone handy who can translate.

However, there's pleasure in being able to use and recognise even just a few words. It's even easier if you have some basic French or Spanish. Pronunciation is reasonably phonetic.

The following letters are pronounced as in English: *b, d, f, l, m, n, t, v*.

For the vowels, pronounce:

a as in English p*a*st;

e has two sounds – as in p*e*st or p*a*ste;

i as in pr*ie*st;

o has two sounds – as in p*o*st or p*o*t;

u as in b*oo*st.

The tricky consonants are:

c as in *ch*ase or *ch*eese before *e* and *i*;

   as in *c*ast, *c*ost or *c*oot before *a, o* or *u*.

g as in *g*ender or *g*enes before *e* and *i*;

   as in *g*arnish, *g*olf or *g*oose before *a, o* or *u*.

z has two sounds – as in mai*ds* or as in ba*ts*.

Some consonants are twinned for special effects:

ch before *e* or *i* becomes hard like a *k*.

gh before *e* or *i* becomes hard as in *gh*etto.

gl before *i* becomes liquid as in bi*lli*ards.

gn before all vowels is pronounced as in o*ni*on.

qu as in *qu*ality.

The Italian language does not use *k, w, x* or *y*.

For the beginner in Italian, we give a starter kit of a few words to show you're trying.

Greetings

Good morning	Buon giorno
Good afternoon	Buon pomeriggio
Good evening	Buona sera
How are you?	Come sta?
Very well, thank you	Benissimo, grazie
Goodbye	Arrivederci!
Good night	Buona notte

The essentials

Yes	Sì
No	No
Please	Per favore
Thank you	Grazie
Don't mention it	Prego
Excuse me! (on bus, etc)	Permesso!
Do you speak English?	Parla inglese?
I don't understand	Non capisco
At what time?	A che ora?

Money

Where is the bank?	Dov'è la banca?
Currency exchange	Cambio
I want to change $50.	Desidero cambiare cinquanta dollari.
How much is this?	Quanto costa questo?
Something cheaper	Qualcosa più a buon mercato
Too expensive!	Troppo caro!

Shopping

Chemist	la farmacia
Doctor	il medico; dottore
Hairdresser	parrucchiere
Post office	ufficio postale
Supermarket	supermercato
Tobacconist	la tabaccheria
I want to buy...	Voglio comprare...
a city map	una cartina della città
some cigarettes	delle sigarette
some stamps	dei francobolli
postcards	cartoline postali
English newspapers	giornali inglesi

LEARN ITALIAN

Sightseeing

Where is the …?	Dov'è … ?
bridge	il ponte
cathedral	la cattedrale
church	la chiesa
museum	il museo
opera house	l'Opera
palace	il palazzo
square	la piazza
station	la stazione
street	la strada
theatre	il teatro
Turn left, right	volti a sinistra, destra
Go straight ahead	vada diritto
Is it open on Sundays?	È aperto la domenica?
When was it built?	Quando fu costuito?

Signs

Aperto	open
Caldo	hot
Chiuso	closed
Donne	ladies
Ascensore	lift/elevator
Entrata	entrance
Freddo	cold
Gabinetto	toilet
Libero	free, vacant
Occupato	occupied
Pericolo	danger
Signori	gents
Silenzio	silence
Spingere	push
Tirare	pull
Uomini	gents
Uscita	exit
Vietato fumare	no smoking
Vietato l'ingresso	no entrance

Days of the week

Monday to Sunday – Lunedì, martedì, mercoledì, gioverdì, venerdì, sabato, domenica.

Today	oggi
Tomorrow	domani
Yesterday	ieri

Months

January to December – gennaio, febbraio, marzo, aprile, maggio, giugno, luglio, agosto, settembre, ottobre, novembre, dicembre.

Numbers

0	zero
1-10	uno, due, tre, quattro, cinque, sei, sette, otto, nove, dieci
11-19	undici, dodici, tredici, quattordici, quindici, sedici, diciasette, diciotto, diciannove
20-29	venti, ventuno, ventidue, ventitre etc.
30-39	trenta, trentuno, trentadue etc.
40-90	quaranta, cinquanta, sessanta, settanta, ottanta, novanta

100	cento	101	centouno
143	centoquarantatre	200	duecento
1000	mille	2000	duemila
1,000,000	un milione		

First, second, third   primo, secondo, terzo

The menu

Please see the next chapter for a food and drink vocabulary.

Chapter Eleven

Eating and drinking

11.1 Café life and dining out

Rome can be enjoyed sitting down. The locals spend much of their leisure at pavement cafés, gossiping and watching the world go by. Favourite drinks are tiny, extra-strong cups of Espresso coffee, or apéritifs like Campari soda.

There is infinite choice of café locations: in 16th-century piazzas, echoing with children at play; in side-streets, friendly as a village pub; at busy cross-roads, providing ringside seats for the cut-and-thrust blood sport of Italian driving.

Food? Just like everywhere else in Italy, there is good eating almost anywhere you go. Restaurants offer a Menu Turistico at fixed all-inclusive prices, and there are fast-food establishments of every type. But Rome has colourful restaurants by the thousand, and it's worth devoting part of your city break to the enjoyment of good food in surroundings that are loaded with atmosphere.

If you go overboard for Italian cuisine with Italian wine, you can have glorious eating at reasonable cost, with enormous choice of restaurants. It's much more fun than eating standard 'international' hotel menus. Don't worry if you cannot speak Italian - just wave and point. But most waiters have basic English.

Italy features three main kinds of restaurant – *osteria*, *trattoria* and *ristorante*, in ascending order of quality and price, though nowadays the distinction is blurring.

If you cannot manage a full meal at lunch-time, there are plenty of chances for snacks. Many bars have a selection of sandwiches called *tramezzini* which have very appetising fillings.

Another type of restaurant/café is called *tavola calda*, which serves simple hot dishes at reasonable price. They are dotted all over Rome. Customers eat standing up – dishes of spaghetti, ravioli or whatever the dish of the day happens to be. It's very handy for a quick lunch, if you don't want a full sit-down meal spread over a couple of hours.

At a pizzeria, you can fill up with a bowl of thick minestrone and a huge pizza that overlaps a dinner plate.

For picnic eating, there is good, cheap fruit – oranges, cherries, melons, peaches, apricots, grapes, fresh figs, according to season. Excellent cheeses, cooked meats and salads help keep outgoings low.

Learn the Italian word *etto*, which means hectogramme or 100 grammes, about four ounces. Fish or steak dishes are frequently priced per *etto*, not per portion. Know the system, and save yourself a nasty shock when the bill comes.

Bar codes

There is something very typically Italian about the snack bars dominated by a massive Espresso machine, gleaming and polished and steaming. On the shelves behind are bottles of every conceivable spirit and liqueur known to European man. These establishments are also useful as a stopping-point for a quick sandwich. At a typical cafeteria, black coffee costs 800 lire; cappuccino, 1,000 lire.

In the mornings from 7 to 11 a.m. you'll find Italians having their breakfasts of cappuccinos and cornettos (croissants). However, if you feel in need of a brandy, you will not be on your own!

For a stand-up drink, you normally pay first at the cash desk (cassa). Take the receipt to the bar, put a 100- or 200-lire coin on top, and tell the barman what you want. The tip ensures rapid service. Standing at the bar is always much cheaper than having drinks and sandwiches served to a table. You're not supposed to buck the system by ordering at the bar, and then sitting down.

DINING OUT

Set menu

A standard 'menu turistico' comprises a flat-rate 3-course meal, usually with a drink such as beer or quarter-litre of wine, service and tax. The price may be reasonable enough, but don't expect any gastronomic delights.

Most restaurants charge 'coperto', which is a cover charge of about 3,000 lire per person. Then there is service which can add 10-20% on the total bill. Tipping is not necessary on top, unless for exceptional service. VAT is added. Keep your restaurant bill, as tax inspectors are making valiant attempts to keep tabs on the catering trade. Within 200 metres of a restaurant, inspectors can ask you to produce your receipt: otherwise, a hefty fine. For the tourist, it's all rather theoretical.

11.2 Guide to the menu

Zuppe e Antipasti	**Soups and Starters**
Gamberetti	Shrimps
Melone con fichi	Melon with figs
Melone con prosciutto	Melon with ham
Misto or frutti di mare	Mixed seafood
Panada	Broth
Zuppa di pesce	Fish soup
Zuppa di fagioli	Bean soup

Risotti e Pasta	**Rice and Pasta dishes**
Asparagi	Risotto with asparagus
Primavera	Risotto with diced fresh vegetables
Nere de seppie	Risotto with cuttlefish in its ink
Bigoli	Dark coloured pasta
Pasta e fagioli	Pasta with white bean soup
Risi e Anguilla	Rice and eel
Risi e bisi	Rice and peas

Pesce e Crostacei	**Fish and shellfish**
Anguilla	Eel
Aringa	Herring
Baccala	Cod

Branzino	Sea bass
Calamari	Squid
Cozze	Mussels
Frutta di mare	Seafood
Gamberelli	Prawns
Granchi	Shrimps
Nasello	Haddock
Ostriche	Oysters
Pesce spada	Swordfish
Salmone	Salmon
Sgombro	Mackerel
Sogliola	Plaice
Sogliola Finta	Sole
Tonno	Tuna
Triglia	Red Mullet
Trota	Trout

Carne	*Meat*
Agnello	Lamb
Anatra/anitra	Duck
Bistecca	Steak
Bistecca de Filetto	Fillet steak
Braciola	Cutlet, chop
Bue	Beef
Coniglio	Rabbit
Coscia	Leg
Cotoletta/Costata	Cutlet/chop
Fagiono	Pheasant
Fegato	Liver
Maiale	Pork
Manzo	Beef
Montone	Mutton
Pollo	Chicken
Prosciutto	Ham
Ragout	Stew
Rognoni	Kidneys
Rosbif	Roast beef
Salsicce	Sausage
Salsicce alla Griglia	Grilled sausage
Selvaggina	Venison
Tacchino	Turkey
Tournedo	Rump steak
Vitello	Veal

DINING OUT

Verdura	*Vegetables*
Aglio	Garlic
Barbabietola/Bietola	Beetroot
Carciofi	Artichokes
Carotte	Carrots
Cavolfiore	Cauliflower
Cetriolo	Cucumber
Cipolle	Onions
Fagioli	Beans
Funghi	Mushrooms
Insalata	Salad
Lattuga	Lettuce
Melanzana	Aubergines
Patate	Potatoes
Peperoni	Peppers
Piselli	Peas
Pomodoro	Tomato
Spinaci	Spinach

Dolci	*Desserts*
Bussolai	Traditional biscuits from Burano
Gelato	Ice cream
Tirami su	Rich dessert soaked in coffee and liqueur, and covered in cream
Zabaglione	Dessert made with egg yolks and Marsala
Zuppa inglese	Trifle

Frutta	*Fruit*
Albicocca	Apricot
Ananas	Pineapple
Anguria	Water melon
Arancia	Orange
Cillege	Cherries
Fragole	Strawberries
Frutta fresca	Fresh fruit
Lamponi	Raspberries
Mela	Apple
Pera	Pear
Pesca	Peach
Pompelino	Grapefruit
Prugna	Plum

Bibite	*Drinks*
Acqua Minerale	Mineral water
Birra	Beer
Caffè	Black coffee
Cappuccino	White coffee
Latte	Milk
Tè	Tea
Vino – rosso / bianco	Wine – red / white

Miscellaneous

Burro	Butter
Formaggio	Cheese
Frittata	Omelette
Gnocchi	Dumplings
Minestra	Soup
Pane	Bread
Salsa	Sauce
Uova	Eggs

11.3 Eating the Roman way

When in Rome, why not eat *alla Romana* – in the Roman style? Here's a selection of typical regional specialities.

Abbacchio – Roast baby lamb, cooked in white wine and with rosemary seasoning

Abbacchio alla cacciatora – Lamb with an anchovy sauce

Broccoli romani – Broccoli in white wine

Cannelloni – Large pasta tubes, stuffed with various meat, and baked in cheese and tomato sauce

Carciofi alla giudia – Artichokes fried crisp in olive oil and lemon juice

Fettuccini – Thin ribbon pasta made with a sauce of egg, butter, Parmesan cheese and anchovy

Piselli al prosciutto – peas slowly cooked with Parma ham and diced bacon

Spaghetti all'amatriciana – with a sauce of fresh tomatoes, bacon and the piquant Pecorino cheese

Spaghetti alla carbonara – with garlic, peppers, bacon, cheese and egg

Saltimbocca – slices of ham and veal, cooked in butter and marsala sauce

Stracciatella – clear soup with beaten egg and cheese

Suppli – rice croquettes stuffed with Mozzarella cheese and minced meat

The local wine list is also worth exploring. Especially try white, dry and palatable wines of the Castelli Romani, Frascati and Colli Albani. The white medium-dry Est! Est! Est! is internationally known, coming from Montefiascone in the north of the Latium region.

The red Cesanese from Olevano or Piglio is smooth and very palatable. A cool Trebbiano from Aprilia in the area of ancient marshes drained centuries ago, is gaining a good reputation. Aleatico and Greghetto from Gradoli, and Sambuca from Viterbo are also excellent. If you are looking for a guarantee of origin and quality, ask for bottles with the DOC label (Denomination of Origin Controlled). They cost a bit more, but are worth it. In thirsty weather, Romans often mix the ordinary open wines with bubbly mineral water.

11.4 Restaurant suggestions

Price guideline

Prices in the listed restaurants may be subject to change; and obviously everyone orders differently. But here's the price grading system:

£	=	under £15
££	=	£15-£25
£££	=	£25+

Trastevere Area

Cross the Tiber to the Trastevere district for colourful, typical restaurants that cheerfully cater for the tourist trade with perambulating musicians and flower-sellers.

During the warmer months you dine outdoors, lingering over a 2-hour meal with a low-cost bottle or two of wine. On cooler evenings, service is indoors.

Sabatini, Piazza S. Maria in Trastevere 16
Tel: 5812026   £££
Famous for seafood. Also famous for prices! Good food, but among Rome's most expensive restaurants. Closed Wednesdays.

La Tana de Noantri, Via della Paglia 1-3
Tel: 5896575   ££
Near Piazza S. Maria. Very popular, excellent food and good value. Typical Roman dishes. Closed Tuesday.

Ivo's Pizzeria, Via San Francesco Ripa
Tel: 5817082   £
Very crowded and lively. The best pizzas in Rome. Closed Tuesday.

Da Cenci, Via della Lungaretta 67
Tel: 582670   ££
Excellent for seafood. Closed Sunday.

Da Meo Pattaca, Piazza dei Mercanti
Tel: 5816198   ££
Lively atmosphere with music and dancing.

La Fraschetta, Via San Francesco Ripa
Very popular trattoria. Good food. Reasonable prices.   ££

Via Veneto/Spanish Steps area

Dal Bolognese, Piazza del Popolo
Tel: 361426   £££
Opening in the evening from 20.30 onwards. Food expensive, but atmosphere excellent.

Grotte Del Piccione, Via della Vite 37
Tel: 6795336   £
Friendly atmosphere. Pizza a speciality. Closed Monday.

Peppone, Via Emilio 60   Tel: 483976
Closed Sunday.

Piccolo Mondo, Via Aurora 39
Tel: 4754595   £££
For special occasions. Very expensive, but food and location make it worthwhile. Closed Sunday and August.

Osteria Marcello, Via Aurora, near Via Veneto £
Good Italian cooking, in lively surroundings.

DINING OUT

Piazza Navona / Pantheon / Campo dei Fiori

Ristorante Via Gigli d'Oro, Via Gigli d'Oro £££
Interesting, excellent cuisine, but rather pricey.

La Fontanella, Largo Fontanella Borghese 86
Excellent, for a special occasion. £££

La Pollarolla, 25 Piazza Pollarolla   Tel: 6541654
Roman specialities. Closed Mon. £

La Carbonara, 23 Piazza Campo dei Fiori £
Lovely setting on one of Rome's oldest squares.
Closed Tue. Tel: 6564783

L'Orso 80, 33 Via dell'Orso   Tel: 6564904
Try the antipasto. Closed Mon. £

Vatican Area

La Fiorentina, Via Andrea Doria 22 Tel: 312310
Good food, but can be expensive. Specializes in
pizzas cooked in a wood-fired oven. Friendly service, very popular. Closed Wed. ££

Taverna Varrone, Via Varrone   Tel: 6530309
Closed Wednesday. ££

Sardegna Inn, Via Candia 60   Tel: 386521
Sardinian specialities. Closed Monday. ££

Taverna di Giovanni   Tel: 6564116
Via del Banco di Santo Spirito
Try their roast lamb speciality. Closed Mon. ££

Termini Station Area

La Grotta Amatriciana, Via Principe Amedeo
(next to Metropole Hotel) £
Good value at a typical Roman-style family run
trattoria.

Scoglio di Frisio, via Merulana 256 ££
Mediterranean-style restaurant, with authentic musicians playing traditional songs. Excellent for fish or
pizzas. Tel: 734619

La Mangrovia, Via Milazzo 6A   Tel: 4952754
Seafood in relaxing surroundings. Closed Sun. ££

Hostaria Fulvimari, Via Principe Amedeo £
Roman specialities; excellent pasta. Closed Sun.

Osteria de Benedetto, Via Vicenza £
Good food at reasonable prices. Closed Sun.

11.5 Cafés and Bars

Can be divided into three categories: luxurious; typical average; and adequate. Most come in the middle category – welcome ports-of-call for visitors who want to relax from sightseeing, make a phone call, have a snack, go to the lavatory, or even have a cup of coffee. You'll find them everywhere.

Antico Café Greco
Via Condotti (near Spanish Steps)
A place where you can join the smart set for afternoon aperitifs. Not to be missed by literary buffs, as it used to be the haunt of Mark Twain, Oscar Wilde and Hans Christian Andersen.

Ice-cream parlours
You cannot visit Rome without sampling an Italian ice-cream. From preference, go to a gelateria (ice-cream parlour), as their product is of much better quality than what is sold by street vendors.

Giolitti, Via Uffici del Vicario 40 (near Piazza Colonna)
This revered ice-cream parlour is probably the most popular in Rome. It gets very busy, but the ice-cream make it more than worthwhile.

Nota Blu, Salita dei Crescenzi 3 (near Pantheon)
What could be better than home-made ice-cream and a table on the pavement in full view of the magnificent Pantheon? Remember it's very expensive to sit outside, but you can linger if you want.

Tre Scalini, Piazza Navona 30
Renowned for its 'tartufo', which is a rich chocolate ice-cream with chocolate chips through it, and topped with whipped cream.

Chapter Twelve
Enjoy the nightlife

12.1 The evening choice

Rome nightlife is generally noisy, gregarious and a friendly affair, especially in the summer months. There is usually a wide variety of outdoor concerts, film shows, fairs and exhibitions. The best way to check night-time events is to buy a local daily – *Il Messagero*, for example. Or study the English-language publication *This Week in Rome*, available at news-stands. *La Repubblica* newspaper carries a very good once-a-week supplement called *Trova-roma*.

Dining out is part of the nightlife. During the warmer months, go to Trastevere – 'across the Tiber'. Wandering around and choosing an outdoor restaurant is part of the local scene, with musicians entertaining from table to table, and flower-sellers adding to the colour. Especially it is festive season in the second half of July, when wine flows extra freely and everyone's having fun.

Another evening, relax with a drink at a characteristic locality like the Piazza Navona, which has all the bubbly atmosphere of a film set.

By night, the ruins, monuments and fountains of Rome take on a more theatrical appearance, thanks to imaginative use of floodlights. If you haven't already thrown your coin into the Trevi Fountain, make that essential pilgrimage after dark. Night-time, the lit-up monument stands out even more dramatically than by day.

It's amusing to watch the coming and going of visitors and the total blocking of the narrow streets around.

Sampling the café life

Nobody minds the traffic dislocation. Time is unimportant. You can extend your stay in pleasant local bars and cafés, absorbing the atmosphere through the open doorways.

Another amusement is the after-dinner stroll along Via Veneto, which formerly was the haunt of 'café society', sitting at outdoor tables that line the pavements and enjoying *la dolce vita*.

The fashionplates of Rome have long since switched allegiance. But Via Veneto is still worth an hour or two's exploration, by night or day to enjoy the atmosphere of Roman pleasure and luxury. The entire S-curved street dates only from 1887, in what formerly was only vineyards and gardens.

For the full luxury treatment, consider Café de Paris or Doney's.

12.2 Opera and concerts

The Teatro dell'Opera is in full song from November to June, and the company then migrates to the deeply impressive setting of the Caracalla Baths for an open-air season in July, August and September.

This gigantic Roman ruin, looming against the stars, makes a spectacular backdrop to the great scenes of Italian opera. Top favourite for Romans and tourists alike is *Aida*.

The seats are hard, so take padding. The night air cools dramatically, so be prepared with a woolly. Intervals are lengthy, and performances continue till past midnight. Have an afternoon siesta, and you won't doze off partway through. Special buses are available for returning to hotel districts.

Tickets for either the Opera House or the Baths are available at the Opera box office at Piazza Beniamino Gigli, 10-13 hrs and 17-19 hrs.

Among the other regular musical events are open-air summer concerts in the Basilica of Maxentius; winter season concerts of the Accademia Nazionale di Santa Cecilia; and winter concerts of the Accademia Filarmònica Romana.

12.3 The night-hawk scene

In the narrow cobbled streets on the small hill next to Santa Maria Maggiore you can find a selection of bars, opening from 8 p.m. onwards. Try the 'Fiddler's Elbow', a popular and reasonably priced Irish bar at Via dell'Olmata 43 (closed Mon).

Behind the Piazza Navona there is a good selection of bars and café-bars. Try 'Jonathan's Angels'.

Later in the evening in Trastevere, there is excellent choice of bars, many with live music.

Nightclubs and Discos

Be careful before entering nightclubs, as some are extremely expensive, though the entrance price normally includes one drink. However, many clubs offer free entrance on Sunday or Wednesday evening.

Vialle Monte dei Testaccio (between Piramide Metro and Testaccio Bridge) is one of the liveliest areas of Rome, where people don't usually go until after midnight.

Radio Londra, Vialle Monte dei Testaccio
   Lively and very popular.
Caffè Latino, Vialle Monte dei Testaccio
   A more relaxed nightclub, featuring live music.
Alibi, Vialle Monte dei Testaccio
   The most popular of Rome's gay nightclubs.
Alien, Via XX Settembre
   Very trendy, quite expensive.
Gilda, Via Mario de'Fiori 97
   High on glamour and price, for jet-setters.

Jazz clubs
Centro Jazz St Louis
   Via del Cardello 13a   Tel: 4745076
Mississippi Jazz Club
   Borgo Angelico 16
Musica Inn
   Lungotevere dei Fiorentini   Tel: 6544934

Chapter Thirteen

Looking at art

13.1 The great monuments

Today, much of Rome is kept under wraps. Large numbers of the monuments of Rome are partly wreathed in scaffolding, thanks to a major clean-up programme which is converting stoneworks to their original gleaming pristine colours.

Just like in London and Paris, it is delightful to discover that there are more colours to public monuments than just coal-black.

But there's a financial problem. Although many of the public buildings are encased in scaffolding, frequently no work is in progress as funds have run out.

To protect non-existent workers against the sun, monuments are draped with green netting like that used for keeping birds off your raspberries. Money gives out before hope. The scaffolding remains, until more money enables the clean-up to continue.

Many of the picture-postcards of Rome were taken before the Great Age of Scaffolding.

Restoration of the Arch of Constantine began in 1979, and work continued for at least another dozen years. Yet the original was built in only three years!

Car exhausts get most of the blame. They have probably inflicted more damage to historic buildings in the postwar years than was done over the centuries by weather and earthquake.

Meanwhile, the municipal rule is that none of the central buildings may be changed on the exterior. Interiors may be modernised, but facades must remain as before.

LOOKING AT ART

Roman rock

The stone most commonly used in Rome is travertine. The name derives from its place of origin – Tivoli, Latin name *tiburtina*, which lies in the hills east of Rome.

Travertine is a white limestone which the Romans employed for their most grandiose buildings, from majestic temples to the Colosseum. These same rocks were quarried for the greatest buildings of the Christian period and of the modern age.

The various kinds of tufo or 'cappellaccio' are related to travertine, but are less resistant and much less attractive.

Buildings in travertine, like those in baked clay brick, were often finished with a plaster called 'pozzolana' which was dug near Rome. This plaster, still much used, gives buildings in Rome their characteristic purplish red colour.

13.2 Art through the ages

The Etruscans (8th to 2nd centuries BC)

In pre-Roman and early-Roman times, a number of independent Etruscan city-states flourished in central Italy. Numerous archaeological sites have been identified mainly between the Rivers Arno and Tiber.

The Etruscans were maritime traders in frequent contact with the Greeks further south. They owed much to Greek civilization.

Etruscan power waned from the 5th century BC, while Rome gradually expanded throughout the region and assimilated the Etruscan culture. Great quantities of artefacts have come from excavations especially within the necropolis sites of the principal Etruscan cities.

Villa Guilia in Rome houses the most important collection of Etruscan finds.

The Gregorian Etruscan Museum in the Vatican comprises another great collection, and there are some richly endowed Etruscan Rooms in the Capitoline Museum.

Roman times (753 BC to 5th century AD)

While the Romans shone as colonisers, military men, administrators and engineers, they mainly relied on the Greeks to set the patterns for art and architecture.

In their construction of bridges, aqueducts, basilicas and other public buildings, the Romans mastered the use of concrete and brick, along with the new technology of the arch. Greek temple-building aesthetics and Roman know-how were combined into great monuments such as the Pantheon and the Colosseum.

As conquerors of Egypt, the Romans sailed home with numerous obelisks for decoration around the city. The Greeks contributed their artistic flair with statuary, which was copied in disciplined style by Roman craftsmen.

Early Middle Ages (4th-11th centuries)

With the triumph of Christianity as the official religion in the 4th century, Roman basilicas were converted into churches. New church building followed the basic theme of a long hall with two aisles and a semi-circular apse at the far end. Decorative themes were imported from Constantinople – the original Byzantium, capital of the Eastern Roman Empire.

Romanesque (11th-12th centuries)

During this period of European stability and prosperity there was a great wave of church building in all the Italian cities. The intense activity led to much innovation in architectural techniques and styles, while artists began to create highly individual works of pictorial and sculptural decoration.

The word 'Romanesque' originally stood for architecture 'in the Roman style', especially in the use of the rounded arch and barrel vaulting. Churches kept mostly to the earlier Christian basilica form with a three-aisled nave, a transept and a semi-circular apse roofed by a half-dome.

Sculpture was confined mainly to reliefs. Interior church decoration was almost entirely in the form of frescoes, following traditions that were well established from Roman and early Christian times.

LOOKING AT ART

Gothic (12th-14th centuries)

A new outlook came through the teachings of St Francis of Assisi (1182-1226) who preached a more gentle and lovable religion in contrast to the former stern austerity. Painters broke loose from the formal conventions of the Byzantine School, with Giotto leading the way to a fresh and life-like style.

In place of the austere Byzantine backgrounds, biblical stories were set in contemporary dress amid local scenery with familiar hills and countryside. Easel painting came into more general use around this time, permitting a more subtle expression of deep emotions.

Meanwhile, Italian gothic monuments provided large wall and ceiling areas for mural decoration. During this period, the principal technique of fresco painting was based on wet plaster – just enough being applied to a working surface that could be finished in a single day's session. Painters had to work fast, before the plaster dried out. Compositions were mapped out in red chalk. Filling in the details was a team effort, with the master craftsman directing the operation.

Among the great names in this technique were Giotto, Taddeo Gaddi and Maso di Banco in Florence, and Pietro Cavallini in Rome.

Renaissance (15th-16th centuries)

The Renaissance or cultural 'rebirth' of the 15th and 16th centuries marked the end of the Middle Ages, with a revolution in thought that rediscovered the creative heritage of classical Greek and Roman philosophy, literature and science.

The revived interest in the classical world opened up new art themes based on Greek and Roman history and mythology. Artists themselves emerged as imaginative creators rather than as mere craftsmen. In the artistic and cultural history of Western Europe, the Renaissance had the deepest possible influence.

Although Giotto was an isolated forerunner, Early Renaissance developed from a generation of artists who worked in Florence at the start of the 15th century. The trend-setters were Donatello for sculpture, Brunelleschi for architecture and Masaccio for painting – later followed in mid-century by Botticelli in Florence and Giovanni Bellini in Venice. Although Florence remained the centre of innovation throughout the 15th century, other schools followed similar lines, especially in Milan, Venice, Padua and Naples.

In a supremely productive period, about 1495-1520, a few artists of great genius – Leonardo da Vinci, Michelangelo, Bramante, Raphael and Titian – brought a High Renaissance style to perfection. Art-loving popes were enthusiastic patrons throughout this time.

Masters of the Italian School

The word 'school' has nothing to do with teaching! It is applied to the artists of different nations, and of groups of painters within one nation. Italian School – a label mainly applied to the Renaissance artists – is sub-divided into regional schools which each had its individual character, reflecting the local environment and taste of the time. Art experts distinguish between about twenty schools of Italian painting, of which Florence, Venice and Siena are among the most important.

Obviously there was an overlap of styles and techniques, especially when artists moved from the patronage of one city to another. But part of the pleasure of looking at Italian paintings comes from recognising this variety between the regional schools.

As the Church was the single most important patron, religious art predominated. Until the late 13th century, Italian art was influenced mainly by Byzantine techniques of working with mosaic. Pictures depicted rather stiff and gloomy characters in the story of Jesus against a formal gold background.

Fresco painting flourished, to reach its perfection during the early 16th century in the hands of Raphael and Michelangelo. Oil painting – invented about 1500 – then took over in popularity.

The great names of the Venetian School were Bellini, Crivelli, Giorgione, Titian, Carpaccio, Palma, Tintoretto, Veronese, Moroni, Zuccarelli,

Guardi and Tiepolo. Their work is characterised by a sensuous beauty which focussed on bodily beauty more than spirituality. Pictures reflect the luxury of 15th-century Church and State, when material prosperity was at its height.

In contrast, the Florentines preferred a soft tenderness in their paintings, compared with the raw vigour of the Venetians. In the use of colour, the Florentine School inclined towards a cooler approach – rose and purple blue compared with the Venetian leaning towards opulent orange.

Late Renaissance and Mannerism (16th-17th centuries)

The sack of Rome in 1527 by the German and Spanish troops of Holy Roman Emperor Charles V marked the temporary end of Papal patronage. Many leading artists moved to other centres in Italy, Spain and France. Meanwhile, in this Late Renaissance period, a new style called Mannerism had evolved, characterised by highly refined grace and elegance. This was the age of Palladio and Caravaggio, Cellini, Tintoretto and Veronese.

Baroque (17th-18th centuries)

By the end of the 16th century, Mannerism had run its course, to be superseded by the highly ornate Baroque style. Caravaggio set the trend in painting, Bernini in sculpture and Borromini in architecture. The main centre of Baroque for most of the 17th century was Rome.

The spectacular style became highly popular throughout the Catholic world, and also among monarchs and other wealthy secular patrons. The style survived into the 18th century, to be replaced in turn by Rococo. Among the leading artists of the period were Bernini, Canaletto, Guardi and Tiepolo. With their passing, the greatest days of Italian painting came to an end.

Chapter Fourteen

Who's who in Art

14.1 The great artists of Rome

Here are some brief notes on some of the leading artists whose work can be seen in Rome, or who influenced the development of Italian art.

Bellini – 1430-1516. Giovanni Bellini was the most talented member of a family of 15th-century artists. He specialised in portraits and large altarpieces, and pioneered the use of oils in preference to tempera (powdered pigments with egg yolk and water). Among his pupils were Giorgione and Titian.

Botticelli – 1445-1510. A highly influential painter of the Early Renaissance, Sandro Botticelli was apprenticed to a goldsmith but turned to painting under the guidance of Fra Filippo Lippi. He also had links with the painter and sculptor Verrocchio, in whose studio Leonardo da Vinci was apprenticed. In 1481 Pope Sixtus IV commissioned him to help decorate the side walls of the newly completed Sistine Chapel. The following decade was the peak of Botticelli's career, with his workshop producing a wide variety of pictures. His influence remained into the next generation, especially through his pupil, Filippino Lippi – the son of his own teacher.

Bramante – 1444-1514. Greatly influenced at first by the 15th-century architecture of Brunelleschi and Alberti, Donate Bramante spent his earlier years in northern Italy. Later he studied Roman monuments, from which came a new synthesis in the tradition of ancient Rome. As the leading architect of the High

Renaissance, Bramante was appointed by Pope Julius II to direct a huge building programme, including the rebuilding of St Peter's. Bramante died before the work was finished, but his vision of a majestic dome in the style of the Pantheon was finally achieved, with modifications by Michelangelo and others. Bramante set the style for church and palace architecture for at least the next century.

Canova – 1757-1822, is rated by some authorities as the greatest sculptor after Michelangelo. He was a leading exponent of Neoclassicism, reviving the basic themes and styles of the ancient Romans. Trained in Venice, he moved to Rome in 1779. His social prestige won him aristocratic patrons in Rome, Venice and London. He was an abstemious bachelor but produced extremely sensuous work: the most famous example is the portrayal of Napoleon's sister, Pauline, semi-nude in the Borghese Gallery.

Caravaggio – 1573-1610. His highly dramatic style of religious painting was combined with intensive use of light and shadow. He arrived in Rome about 1590, but his most creative period was from 1597 until he fled the city in 1606 after committing murder. Although fiercely independent, taking on no pupils or assistants, Caravaggio had many followers in the new baroque idiom, which spread to France and Flanders, especially through Rubens who studied his techniques.

Cellini – 1500-1571. A typical 'Renaissance man', Benvenuto Cellini was equally versatile as a writer, sculptor, goldsmith or architect. Born in Florence, he learned his gold-working skills from his father, who doubled as a musician. In his early years – between 1516 and 1540 – Cellini moved around the principal cities of Italy, working for the papacy and for aristocratic patrons.

Donatello – 1386-1466. As a contemporary of Ghiberti, Donatello was a leading Florentine sculptor of the early Renaissance. He covered every medium of sculpture, lively and full of character.

Giotto – 1266-1337 – was the great pioneer of Renaissance art in Florence. As a 10-year-old shepherd boy he was 'discovered' by Cimabue, who trained him in his studio.

Leonardo da Vinci – 1452-1519. Born near Florence, he showed artistic talent from an early age. Leonardo entered the painters' guild in 1472, and his earliest masterworks date from then. From 1482, Leonardo worked 18 years for the ruling Sforza family of Milan – producing court portraits, arranging festivals, designing military fortifications and painting *The Last Supper*. During that period he undertook wide-ranging scientific and technical studies in anatomy, biology, map-making, mathematics and physics. In 1513 he returned to Rome for a three-year stint, mainly devoted to theoretical research. Leonardo must rate as the most creative mind of the age – a true Renaissance man.

Lorenzo Lotto – 1480-1556. A Venetian painter, Lotto worked in many Italian cities, but was particularly exposed to the High Renaissance style of Florence and Rome. He worked for several years with other artists, decorating the apartments of Pope Julius II – a task later completed by Raphael.

Michelangelo – 1475-1564. Greatest of the Renaissance artists, Michelangelo was a giant in painting, sculpture and architecture. In adolescence he came under the wing of the Medici family. He rapidly made his mark with marble statues carved while in his twenties, including the *Pietà* in St Peter's. Called to Rome in 1505 to undertake a stupendous tomb for Pope Julius II, he was sidetracked into the even bigger assignment of portraying the biblical history of humanity on the Sistine Chapel ceiling. That project (1508-1512) must rate as his supreme achievement, changing the entire course of Western art. In later years his style changed. The artistic ferment is exemplified by his *Last Judgement* in the Sistine Chapel (1536-41). In the final years of his long and productive life, Michelangelo returned to his first love, sculpture. He died aged 88.

ART AND MYTH

Perugino – 1445-1523. This eminent Renaissance painter probably trained in Florence where a number of his works are located. In 1481 he was leader of the project to decorate the walls of the Sistine Chapel, together with Botticelli and Ghirlandaio. His *Christ Giving the Keys to St Peter* survives, though his frescoes on the end wall were replaced by Michelangelo's *Last Judgement*. In his later years Perugino's large workshop of students and assistants included Raphael.

Raphael – 1483-1520. Among the greatest painters of the High Renaissance, Raphael started young, apprenticed at age 11 to Perugino. By the age of 20 he was producing great masterpieces. Living in Florence from 1504 to 1508, he absorbed much from Leonardo da Vinci and other masters. Many examples of this highly productive period are treasured in the world's leading galleries.

At age 25 he was commissioned by Pope Julius II to supervise the decoration of the State Rooms in the Vatican Palace. Simultaneously Raphael produced paintings for many private patrons. In 1514 he became chief architect of St Peter's Basilica. Although his designs never came to fruition, other architectural work in Rome still survives.

Tintoretto – 1518-1594 – was a Venetian painter on the grand scale. His themes ranged from historic battle scenes to religious and mythological subjects. Two sons and a daughter were part of the production line of pupils and assistants. Tintoretto's work was Mannerist in style, combining the colour techniques of Titian with the drawing of Michelangelo.

Titian – 1488-1576. During his long and productive life, Titian created hundreds of masterly portraits and religious and mythological paintings.

He studied in Venice under the brothers Gentile and Giovanni Bellini, but the greatest influence came from Giorgione, with whom he was closely associated. Titian adopted many of Giorgione's innovations in colour and brush techniques, and in his poetic interpretation of figures and landscape.

14.2 Who's who among the gods

From the Renaissance onwards, artists turned more frequently to subjects based on classical Roman mythology, which often had been adapted from the pantheon of the Greeks. Here's a short list of the more popular characters.

Apollo – or Phoebus, the sun god; the god of prophesy, music, song and the arts. Protector of flocks and herds.

Bacchus – Dionysos – god of vegetation, and the fruits of the trees, especially wine.

Cupid – the Greek Eros – the lovers' favourite.

Diana – otherwise known as Artemis – deity of the chase; goddess of the moon, protectress of the young. Sister of Apollo.

Fortuna – the Greek Tyche – personifying fortune, usually depicted holding a rudder, or with a globe or cornucopia.

Juno – Hera among the Greeks – the good wife of Jupiter.

Jupiter – Zeus – greatest of the Olympian Gods; father of both gods and men.

Mars – father of the twin founders of Rome, he was favoured with several temples to his name.

Medusa – one of the three Gorgon sisters – lost her head to Perseus, blood everywhere.

Mercury – Hermes – messenger of the gods, who usually wore a travelling hat, golden sandals, and a purse. Mercury was patron of merchants, thieves, artists, orators and travellers.

Minerva – based on the Greek Athena, goddess of war and wisdom; patroness of agriculture, industry and the arts.

Nemesis – the fatal divinity, measuring out happiness and unhappiness.

Neptune – Poseidon – god of the sea, and responsible for earthquakes.

Venus – Aphrodite – goddess of love and beauty. Sometimes appears with a sea-horse or dolphin. Julius Caesar claimed her as an ancestor.

Chapter Fifteen

Travel hints

15.1 Money and Banking

The Italian unit of currency is the lira (plural lire).

Coins	Notes
50 lire	1,000 lire
100 lire	2,000 lire
200 lire	5,000 lire
500 lire	10,000 lire
	50,000 lire
	100,000 lire

The symbol used for marking prices is either a letter 'L', or similar to the pound sterling sign – £.

Unless you're very fast at mental arithmetic, Italian lire are confusing for the first day or two. unless it's a handy equivalent like 2,500 lire to the pound. Suggestion: before departure, check the current exchange rate, and list out some conversions on a postcard, as a handy crib.

There is often a shortage of small change, and telephone tokens (worth 200 lire), sweets or stamps may be used to make up the deficiency.

Changing Money

Take a starter kit of a bundle of lire, to tide you over the first day or two in Italy, especially if you arrive at weekends. There are exchange desks at the arrival airport or railway terminus. Banks are normally open 8.30 a.m. till 1.20 p.m., and for a variable hour in the afternoon, Monday till Friday, closed weekends. Rates can vary from bank to bank, so it's worth comparing their display panels.

A flat commission of up to 3000 lire on Traveller Cheques makes it uneconomic to change little and often. Some Exchange Bureaux keep longer hours, and take a bigger slice of your money. Larger hotels can also oblige, but give even more unfriendly rates.

Remember to take your passport when changing money.

Personal Cheques & Eurocheques

Backed by the appropriate banker's card, Eurocheques are among the simplest and most acceptable means of payment. These must be specially ordered from your bank, but are well worth it, as you can then write cheques in the local currency. They can also be used in UK.

The Eurocheque card allows you to cash up to £120 on each cheque, and is valid for making payments to shops, hotels and restaurants that display the 'ec' sign. Many places also accept normal cheques up to £50 if backed by a banker's card.

Bank opening hours:

Generally, Mon-Fri 8.30-13.30 hrs. Some banks re-open 14.45-15.45 hrs.
Exchange Bureaux (Cambio): at Termini Station open 8.30-21 hrs (but may vary in winter). Other exchange bureaux open 9-13 and 15.30-19.30 hrs. Some close Saturdays.

Credit Cards

Access, Visa, American Express and Diners Club are widely accepted at shops and restaurants. At some banks you can withdraw cash, but it's often inconvenient. Don't over-rely on credit cards for getting cash, though automatic cash machines are becoming more prevalent.

Reconverting cash

Normally, convert any surplus lire back into sterling or dollars at the departure airport. Avoid taking 50,000 and 100,000 lire notes back into the UK, as banks may refuse to change them and certainly will give a lower rate.

15.2 Security

Pickpockets

Just like elsewhere in Europe, Italy's main cities have their quota of hardworking pickpockets who specialise in the tourist trade. Their guess is that holidaymaker handbags or wallets will contain an above-average supply of currency, traveller cheques and credit cards. The light-fingered gentry are not necessarily bent Italians. International teams work the season, often looking just like other tourists.

Be careful in crowded places, especially if travelling by bus or Metro. Pickpockets often work in pairs, taking advantage of crowds to jostle their victims while stealing a purse or wallet. In narrow side-streets, scooter riders have perfected a mobile bag-snatching technique as they swoop past.

Like a Mediterranean version of *Oliver*, gipsy kids are among the most active pickpockets. A member of the gang thrusts a cardboard sign under your nose and pleads for alms. At a lower level, confederates cluster round to fish through your pockets and handbag. A gipsy Fagin lurks watchfully in the background. If you're approached, take evasive action, clutch your belongings and yell.

There's no need to be suspicious of all strangers. But don't make things easy for crooks.

Never carry a wallet in your hip pocket. Keep handbags fastened and held securely. In a café or restaurant, don't hang camera or handbag over the back of your chair.

Minimise any potential loss by leaving the bulk of your valuables in the safety deposits available to hotel guests. Keep a separate record of traveller-cheque numbers, and also of credit-card details of where to notify in case of loss. It also helps to have a photo-copy of your passport details.

If you have anything stolen, report to the nearest police station and obtain an official declaration of theft, required for insurance reclaim. If you're on a package tour with insurance cover, contact the travel-agency representative for advice on making a 'Loss Report' to send with your claim form.

Police Headquarters – Questura at Via Genova 2
This police station never closes. English speakers are available 24 hours. Tel: 4686. Nearest Metro – Repubblica.

If your passport has gone missing, once you have the police report you should go to the British Consulate (adjoining the British Embassy at Via XX Settembre 80/A) taking two passport size photographs. The Consulate will issue a temporary passport to get you home.

Female harrassment

Of course, it does exist. Best advice is to ignore the persistent overtures, until the idiots get tired of the game and try elsewhere. Otherwise, say "NO!" in loud English. It means the same in Italian. You could also respond in basic Anglo-Saxon, which would be equally well understood.

15.3 Postal and phone services

Post Offices (Ufficio Postale) handle telegrams, mail and money transfers, and some have public telephones.

Opening hours are generally Mon-Fri 8.15-14.00 hours; Sat 8.30-12.00. The system gets low marks for efficiency, and queues are long. Air mail seems to travel by slow pigeon, and you'll easily race postcards home.

The Main Post Office is located on Piazza Silvestro (near corner of Via del Corso and Via del Tritone) – open Mon-Fri 8.30-20.00 hrs; Sat 8.30-18.00 hrs. Closed Sunday and Holy days.

The Vatican post office has a much higher reputation for efficiency, but you'll need Vatican stamps if you post in the blue mail-boxes of Vatican City.

Stamps are also sold at tobacconists' (tabaccheria) with a 'T' sign above the door. They're a lot more helpful if you buy some postcards at the same time! Likewise, some hotel desks carry a stamp supply.

Stamps are 'francobolli' in Italian. Post boxes are red, and non-local mail should be posted in the slot marked 'altre destinazioni'.

TRAVEL HINTS

Phoning home

Making long distance and international calls from hotels is an expensive luxury! Instead, go to the nearest office of TELECOM. There's a line of cabins, and a queue. When your turn comes, the counter clerk will tell you which booth number to use. The Post Office in Piazza Silvestro has a telephone section – called the ASST office – right next door, open 8 a.m. till midnight.

● Dial 00 for International Exchange, and wait for a tone change.

● Dial 44 (the international code for UK) plus the appropriate STD town dialling code, minus the first zero; then the local number. Thus, to call Barnsley (code 01226) 12345, dial 0044 1226 12345. Other country codes are: USA and Canada 1; Australia 61; New Zealand 64; Eire 353.

● Afterwards, you return to the desk to pay for the telephone call at the regular cost with no mark-ups. Calls are cheaper after 11 p.m. or before 8 a.m., and throughout the weekend from 14.30 hrs on Saturday.

Phone cards called *scheda*, costing 5,000 or 10,000 lire at Telecom offices and tobacconists, are the best way of making international phone calls. When you buy a new card, tear off the corner where it says *stracciare* or *strappare* - otherwise the card will not completely enter the slot. The residual value shows on the screen. Long distance calls can be made from telephone boxes with a yellow disc and the word 'teleselezione' or 'interurbana'.

Coin boxes: For local calls, you'll need two 100-lire coins or one 200-lire coin for the modern call box; or occasionally a *gettone* (token) which costs 200 lire at a bar. Lift receiver, insert the coins or token and dial. 'Guasto' means broken or out of order.

Reverse charge calls to UK or North America can be placed by inserting your basic 200 lire, and dialling 172 followed by the national code. You then negotiate your reverse-charge number with the

operator in the home country. If you come equipped
with a British Telecom chargecard – or AT&T for
North America – the cost can be charged to your
home number.

To call Rome from other countries, the international code is 39-6. Thus, from Britain, dial 010-
39-6 followed by the local number in Rome. From
North America, dial 011-39-6 etc.

Local Rome phone numbers can be weird, anything from four to eight digits long. Thus, the Vatican switchboard number is 6982. Just think of
whisky, VAT 69, to get you started.

15.4 Medical

As part of EEC reciprocal health arrangements, UK
visitors can get all medical services that are available to Italians. Before departure from Britain, ask
your local Department of Health and Social Security
(DHSS) office for the "Medical Costs Abroad"
leaflet no. SA30. Fill out the form CM1 and send it
to the DHSS, who will supply form E111 to take
with you. It's probably not worth the effort for
minor ailments, but would be most useful if anything major happened.

Should you require a doctor, contact your hotel
concierge and ask him to call one.

If you have holiday or medical insurance, get
receipts both from the doctor and the chemist, so as
to make any necessary reclaim. If you're on a
package tour, and sizeable funds are needed to
cover medical expenses, contact your travel-agency
rep for advice.

If mosquitoes normally have you for supper,
bring some repellent. Biting insects are most active
in July and August. To ensure peaceful sleep, you
can outwit night-flying insects by keeping bedroom
windows closed and air conditioning switched on.
It's also worth packing an electrically-operated mos-
quito kit, which can be remarkably effective.

A combination of hot weather, iced drinks and
different food can cause tummy problems. If the
bug hits, doctors advise drinking plenty of fruit

juice - such as lemon or orange - or bottled water with a twitch of sugar and salt (to counter dehydration). Continue eating normally.

Among the pharmaceuticals, Lomotil, Imodium and Arrêt are usually effective, and one of those may be worth packing. Local doctors can provide stronger preparations if necessary.

You have to be desperate, to use the facilities in some of the wayside cafés which you may wish to visit in a hurry. Sometimes the gap between utter misery and fulfillment is measured by a few sheets of toilet paper. Always carry a few spares in your holdall, in case of emergencies.

Chemists are open only during normal shop hours, but a window sign indicates the nearest night or Sunday-opening chemist ('farmacia').

15.5 What to wear and pack

Casual dress is OK for tourist Rome, though you may prefer something more formal for any up-market evening dining or a visit to the Opera House. Most likely you'll be on your feet most of the day, so forget about high heels. Comfortable flat footwear is much better.

To enter St Peter's - and many other churches and catacombs - you should be soberly dressed: no shorts; no above-the-knee skirts; no sleeveless dresses (though women can get by with a scarf draped over shoulders). Otherwise you will be politely turned away.

Pack binoculars or opera glasses for better viewing of mosaics and paintings - in the Sistine Chapel, for instance.

If you want to use any electric gadgets, pack a plug adaptor. Rome is on 220 volts, but uses the Continental-type 2-pin plug.

Don't worry if your cosmetic, pharmaceutical or film supplies run out. All the major brands are readily available.

However, take rather more camera film than you'd normally carry to other European destinations. Rome is rich in photo subjects, and it's hard to resist taking still more pictures. Why waste time buying more film on the spot, at prices that are higher than back home?

In the expectation of buying some stylish Italian clothing, many visitors travel out light in their luggage to leave room for the loot.

It's also worth packing ultra-light if you are fending for yourself between airport or station and your hotel. Otherwise the cost of Roman taxis and porters can be high.

15.6 Home news

The English-language newspapers which arrive first in Rome are *The Guardian, Financial Times*, *International Herald Tribune* and *The Wall Street Journal* – all printed on the Continent. Other London newspapers and magazines normally arrive by afternoon, and cost about double the UK price.

Most of the larger hotels are now equipped to receive satellite TV, and can offer 24-hour choice of CNN, Sky News and similar programmes.

If your holiday would be ruined without important home news like up-to-date Test Match scores, it's worth packing a short-wave radio, to catch the regular on-the-hour news bulletins of the BBC World Service. The best wave-lengths for Rome are:

Early morning – 15575 on 19m band; 9410 on 31-meter band; 6195 on 49m band.
Daytime – 12095 on 25-meter band; 15070 on 19m band; 17640 on 17m band.
Evening – 9410 on 31m band; 6195 on 49m band; 7325 on 41m band.

Reception varies greatly according to time and location. Reception can be greatly improved with an external aerial. A length of wire dangling over your balcony can make all the difference.

Medium or Long Wave cannot be relied upon, but you could always try your luck on 648 Medium Wave or 198 Long Wave.

Chapter Sixteen
Quick reference

16.1 Public holidays

1 January	New Year's Day
6 January	Epiphany
25 April	Liberation Day, 1945
Easter Monday	
1 May	May Day
15 August	Assumption
1 November	All Saints
8 December	Immaculate Conception
25 December	Christmas Day
26 December	St Stephen's Day

Rome also holds June 29 as a local holiday for Saints Peter and Paul.

Be prepared for 3-day closure of banking and other services when any of these holidays makes a bridge with the weekend.

16.2 Whom to contact

Emergency

Police – Fire Brigade – Ambulance –	**Dial 113**
Medical Assistance	338 3730
First aid, ambulance	5510

Lost Property

To claim any objects handed in to the Lost Property office, you must have a copy of the declaration made to the police. Phone enquiries are usually a waste of breath.

Municipal Lost Property Office   Tel: 581604
Via Nicolo Bettoni 1 (in Trastevere district, a few
blocks north of Testaccio Bridge).
Open: Mon-Sat 9-12 hrs.

ATAC – for losses on city transport
    Via Volturno 65 (near Termini Station)

Embassies and Consulates
British – Via XX Settembre 80A
                         Tel: 4825441; 4825551
American – Via Veneto 119A   Tel: 46741
Canadian – Via G.B. de Rossi 27   Tel: 445981
Australian – Via Alessandria 215   Tel: 852721
New Zealand – Via Zara 28   Tel: 4402928
Irish – Piazza Campitelli 3   Tel: 6979121

Tourist Information Offices
Ente Nazionale per il Turismo (ENIT)
    Via Marghera 2 (near Termini Station)
    Information   Tel: 4971222; 4971282; 4971646
EPT di Roma, (Rome Provincial Tourist Office)
    via Parigi 5   Tel: 4883748
    in Termini Station entrance hall
                         Tel: 4871270; 4824078
    Leonardo da Vinci Airport, arrivals hall
                         Tel: 65010255
Vatican Information   Tel: 6984866; 6984466
    Office on south side of St Peter's Square
Compagnia Italiano Turismo (CIT)
    Piazza della Repubblica 64   Tel: 47941
    Termini Station   Tel: 474092
ATAC (transport information & maps) Tel: 49951
    Piazza dei Cinquecento, facing Termini Station

More Information
For any further holiday information before you
travel, contact the Italian State Tourist Office
(ENIT for short):

London – 1 Princes Street, London W1R 8AY.
Tel: (0171) 408-1254. Mon-Fri 9-14.30 hrs.
New York – 630 Fifth Avenue, Suite 1565, New
York, NY 10111. Tel: (212) 245-4822/4.

REFERENCE

Chicago – 500 North Michigan Avenue, Chicago, IL 60611. Tel: (312) 644-0990/1.
Los Angeles – 12400 Wilshire Blvd., Suite 550, Los Angeles, CA 90025. Tel: (310) 820-0098.
Montreal – 1 Place Ville Marie, Suite 1914, Montreal, Quebec. Tel: (514) 866-7667.

In Rome itself, try to acquire or borrow from your hotel a free publication called "un Ospite a Roma" – "A Guest in Rome" – packed with current timings and prices in English for museums and galleries, concerts, exhibitions, events, etc.